Mike McGrath

C#
Programming

in
easy steps

Second Edition

In easy steps is an imprint of In Easy Steps Limited
16 Hamilton Terrace · Holly Walk · Leamington Spa
Warwickshire · United Kingdom · CV32 4LY
www.ineasysteps.com

Second Edition

Notice of Liability
Every effort has been made to ensure that this book contains accurate
and current information. However, In Easy Steps Limited and the
author shall not be liable for any loss or damage suffered by readers
as a result of any information contained herein.

Trademarks
All trademarks are acknowledged as belonging to their respective
companies.

In Easy Steps Limited supports The Forest Stewardship Council (FSC),
the leading international forest certification organization. All our titles
that are printed on Greenpeace approved FSC certified paper carry the
FSC logo.

MIX
Paper from
responsible sources
FSC® C020837

Printed and bound in the United Kingdom

ISBN 978-1-84078-906-5

Contents

1 Getting started

Welcome to the exciting world of C# programming. This chapter introduces the Visual Studio Integrated Development Environment and shows you how to create a real Windows application.

The source code of all examples in this book is available for free download at www.ineasysteps. com/resource-center/ downloads

If you don't achieve the result illustrated in any example, simply compare your code to that in the original example files you have downloaded to discover where you went wrong.

Introducing C#

The introduction of the Microsoft .NET framework at the Professional Developers Conference in July 2000 also saw Microsoft introduce a new programming language called C# (pronounced "see-sharp"). The name was inspired by musical notation where a # sharp symbol indicates that a written note should be a semitone higher in pitch. This notion is similar to the naming of the C++ programming language where the ++ symbol indicates that a written value should be incremented by 1.

● C# is designed to be a simple, modern, general-purpose, object-oriented programming language, borrowing key concepts from several other languages – most notably the Java programming language. Consequently, everything in C# is a class "object" with "properties" and "methods" that can be employed by a program.

● C# is an elegant and "type-safe" programming language that enables developers to build a variety of secure and robust applications. You can use C# to create Windows client applications, XML web services, distributed components, client-server applications, database applications, and much, much more.

● C# is specifically designed to utilize the proven functionality built into the .NET framework "class libraries". Windows applications written in C# therefore require the Microsoft .NET framework to be installed on the computer running the application – typically, an integral component of the system.

The Microsoft .NET Framework

Each version of the Microsoft .NET framework includes a unified set of class libraries and a virtual execution system called the Common Language Runtime (CLR). The CLR allows the C# language and the class libraries to work together seamlessly.

To create an executable program, source code written in the C# language is compiled by the C# Compiler into Intermediate Language (IL) code. This is stored on disk, together with other program resources such as images, in an "assembly". Typically, the assembly will have a file extension of .exe or .dll. Each assembly contains a "manifest" that provides information about that program's security requirements.

When a C# program is executed, the assembly is loaded into the Common Language Runtime (CLR), and the security requirements specified in its assembly manifest are examined. When the security requirements are satisfied, the CLR performs Just-In-Time (JIT) compilation of the IL code into native machine instructions. The CLR then performs "garbage collection", exception handling, and resource management tasks before calling upon the operating system to execute the program:

Just-In-Time compilation is also known as "Dynamic Translation".

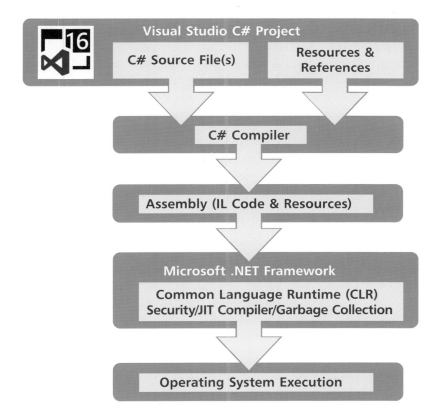

Just-In-Time compilation occurs during program execution, rather than prior to its execution.

As language interoperability is a key feature of the Microsoft .NET framework, the IL code generated by the C# Compiler can interact with code generated by the .NET versions of other languages such as Visual Basic and Visual C++. The examples throughout this book demonstrate Visual C# program code.

Installing Visual Studio

In order to create Windows applications with the C# programming language, you will first need to install a Visual Studio Integrated Development Environment (IDE).

Microsoft Visual Studio is the professional development tool that provides a fully Integrated Development Environment for Visual Basic, Visual C++, Visual J#, and Visual C#. Within its IDE, code can be written in Visual Basic, C++, J#, or the C# programming language to create Windows applications.

Visual Studio Community edition is a streamlined version of Visual Studio, specially created for those people learning programming. It has a simplified user interface and omits advanced features of the professional edition to avoid confusion. C# code can be written within the **Code Editor** of either version of the Visual Studio IDE to create Windows applications.

Both Visual Studio and Visual Studio Community provide an IDE for C# programming but, unlike the fully-featured Visual Studio product, the Visual Studio Community edition is completely free and can be installed on any system meeting the following minimum requirements:

The **New** icon pictured above indicates a new or enhanced feature introduced with the latest version of C# and Visual Studio.

Component	Requirement
Operating system	Windows 10 (version 1703 or higher) Windows Server 2016 or 2019 Windows 8.1 (with update 2919355) Windows 7 Service Pack 1 Windows Server 2012 R2
CPU (processor)	1.8 GHz or faster
RAM (memory)	2 GB (8 GB recommended)
HDD (hard drive)	Up to 210 GB available space
Video Card	Minimum resolution of 1280 x 720 Optimum resolution of 1366 x 768

The Visual Studio Community edition is used throughout this book to demonstrate programming with the C# language, but the examples can also be recreated in Visual Studio. Follow the steps opposite to install the Visual Studio Community edition.

1 Open your web browser and navigate to the Visual Studio Community download page – at the time of writing this can be found at **visualstudio.microsoft.com/downloads**

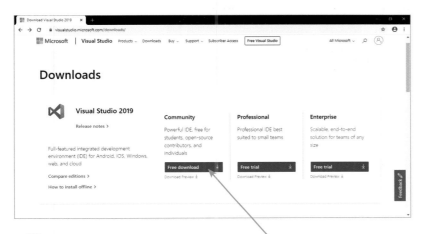

Choosing a different destination folder may require other paths to be adjusted later – it's simpler to just accept the suggested default.

2 Click the button in the Community edition section to download a **vs_community** installer file

3 Click on the ◢◣ **vs_community** file to run the installer

4 Accept the suggested installation location, then click **Next**

5 Choose the two C# options below for installation

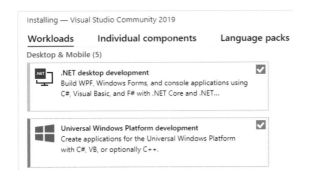

You can re-run the installer at a later date to add or remove features.

6 Click the **Install** button at the bottom-right of the installer to begin the download and installation process

Exploring the IDE

1 Go to your apps menu, then select the Visual Studio 2019 menu item added there by the installer:

2 Sign in with your Microsoft account, or register an account then sign in, to continue

3 See a default **Start Page** appear where recent projects will be listed alongside several "Get started" options

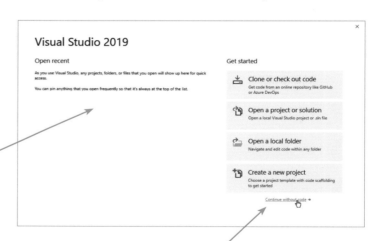

In the future your recent projects will be listed here so you can easily reopen them.

4 For now, just click the link to **Continue without code** to launch the Visual Studio application

The Visual Studio Integrated Development Environment (IDE) appears, from which you have instant access to everything needed to produce complete Windows applications – from here you can create exciting visual interfaces, enter code, compile and execute applications, debug errors, and much more.

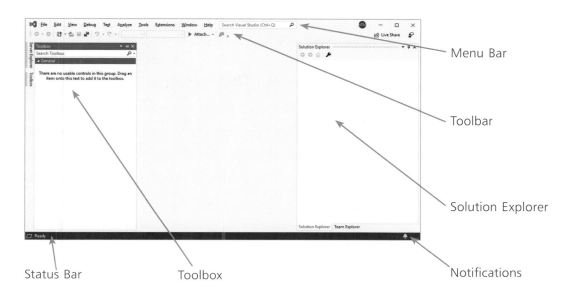

Menu Bar

Toolbar

Solution Explorer

Notifications

Status Bar

Toolbox

Visual Studio IDE components

The Visual Studio IDE initially provides these standard features:

- **Menu Bar** – Where you can select actions to perform on all your project files and to access Help. When a project is open, extra menus of Project and Build are shown in addition to the default menu selection of File, Edit, View, Debug, Test, Analyze, Tools, Extensions, Window, and Help.

- **Toolbar** – Where you can perform the most popular menu actions with just a single click on their associated shortcut icons.

- **Toolbox** – Where you can select visual elements to add to a project. Click the Toolbox side bar button to see its contents. When a project is open, "controls" such as Button, Label, CheckBox, RadioButton, and TextBox are shown here.

- **Solution Explorer** – Where you can see at a glance all the files and resource components contained within an open project.

- **Status Bar** – Where you can read the state of the current activity being undertaken. When building an application, a "Build started" message is displayed here, changing to a "Build succeeded" or "Build failed" message upon completion.

Hot tip

To change the color, choose the **Tools**, **Options** menu then select **Environment**, **General, Color Theme**.

13

GettingStarted

The source code of all examples in this book is available for free download at www.ineasysteps. com/resource-center/downloads

The default location for Visual Studio projects is a **C:\Users*username*\ source\repos** directory.

If the Code Editor window does not open automatically, click the **Program.cs** file icon in Solution Explorer to open the Code Editor.

Starting a Console project

1 On the Menu Bar, click **File**, **New**, **Project...**, or press the **Ctrl** + **Shift** + **N** keys, to open the "New Project" dialog box

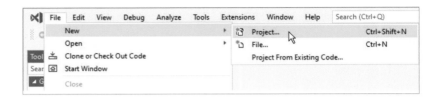

2 In the "Create a new project" dialog box, select the **C# Console App (.NET Core)** item and click **Next**

3 On the next dialog, enter a project name and location then click the **Create** button

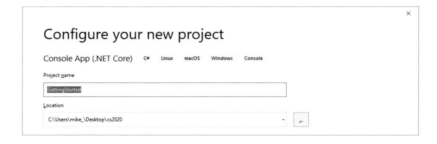

Visual Studio now creates your new project and loads it into the IDE. A **Code Editor** window appears, containing default skeleton project code generated by Visual Studio.

4 Drag the **Code Editor** window tab to undock the **Code Editor** window from the Visual Studio IDE frame

The undocked window title displays the project name, and
the tab displays the file name of the code as "Program.cs".

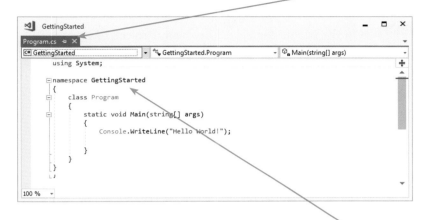

The code **namespace** is declared using your chosen project name –
in this case it's "GettingStarted".

Hot tip

You can drag the title
bar of any window to
undock that window
from the Visual Studio
IDE frame. When
dragging, you can drop
a window on the "guide
diamond" (shown below)
to dock the window in
your preferred position.

5 Select the **View, Solution
Explorer** menu to open a
Solution Explorer window,
to discover all the items in
your project

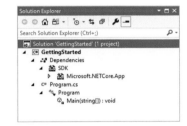

6 Select
the **View,
Properties**
menu to open
a **Properties**
window, then
select any
item in the
**Solution
Explorer** window to see its properties appear in the
Properties window

The **Code Editor** window is where you write C# code to create
an application. The Visual Studio IDE has now gathered all the
resources needed to build a default Console application. You can
click the **Start** button on the toolbar to see Visual Studio build
this application, but it will do nothing until you add some code.

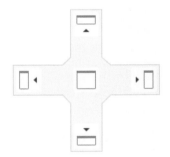

Hot tip

Alternatively, you can
run applications using
the **Debug, Start
Debugging** menu
options, or press the **F5**
shortcut key.

15

Writing your first program

In order to create a working Console application you need to add C# code to the default skeleton project code generated by the Visual Studio IDE:

Hello

1 On the Menu Bar, click **File**, **New**, **Project**, or press the **Ctrl** + **Shift** + **N** keys, to open the "New Project" dialog box

2 In the "New Project" dialog box, select the **Installed**, **Visual C#**, **Console App (.NET Core)** item

3 Enter a project name of your choice in the **Name** field – in this case the project name will be "Hello"

4 Click on the **OK** button to create the new project and see the **Code Editor** display the default skeleton project code

5 Position the cursor at the end of the line that reads **Console.WriteLine("Hello World!") ;**

6 Hit Enter to add a new line, then precisely type this code **Console.WriteLine("Press Any Key To Continue...") ;**

7 Hit **Enter** to add another new line, then type this code **Console.ReadKey( ) ;**

Hot tip

As you type the code, a suggestion box will appear. This is the "IntelliSense" feature. You can select an item then insert it into your code by pressing the Tab key or the Spacebar.

Hot tip

The **Main()** method is automatically called whenever a C# program is run – to execute the instructions contained within its **{ }** braces.

16

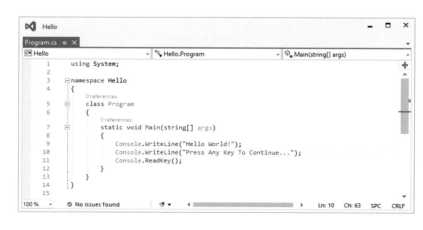

```csharp
using System;

namespace Hello
{
    class Program
    {
        static void Main(string[] args)
        {
            Console.WriteLine("Hello World!");
            Console.WriteLine("Press Any Key To Continue...");
            Console.ReadKey();
        }
    }
}
```

8 Now, select **File**, **Save Hello**, or press the **Ctrl + S** keys, to save the completed C# Console application

9 Then, select the ▶ Start ▾ **Start** button on the Toolbar, or press the **F5** key, to build and run the application

```
C:\Users\mike_\Desktop\cs2020\Hello\bin\Debug\netcoreapp3.1\Hello.exe        —   □   ×
Hello World!
Press Any Key To Continue...
_
```

A Console window like the one shown above should now appear, displaying a traditional programming greeting.

10 Hit **Enter**, or click the ■ **Stop** button, to close the application and see the Console window disappear

Code analysis
Examination of the code helps to understand what is happening:

● **using System ;** This is a <u>directive</u> allowing the **System.**Console class object to be written without the **System.** prefix.

● **namespace Hello { }** This is a <u>declaration</u> that creates a unique namespace wrapper in which to enclose your program.

● **class Program { }** This declaration creates a "Program" class in which to create your own program properties and methods.

● **static void Main(string[ ] args) { }** This declaration creates a standard **Main( )** method in which to write your C# code.

● **Console.WriteLine("Hello World!") ;** This is a <u>statement</u> that calls upon the **WriteLine( )** method of the Console class to output text enclosed in quote marks within its parentheses.

● **Console.ReadKey( ) ;** This statement calls upon the **ReadKey( )** method of the Console class to wait for any key to be pressed.

To edit the default Console window colors and font, right-click its window Titlebar and choose **Properties**. For clarity, all other Console window screenshots in this book feature Lucida Console 14-pixel **Font** in black **Screen Text** on a white **Screen Background**.

Code listed throughout this book is colored to match the default syntax highlight colors of the Visual Studio Code Editor for easy recognition.

Calling the **ReadKey( )** method is a little trick to keep the Console window open until you press any key. Without this statement, the application would output its message then immediately exit.

17

Following the rules

As with all programming languages, C# has a number of syntax rules that must be precisely followed to ensure the code is correctly formatted for the C# compiler to clearly understand:

- **Case-sensitivity** – C# is a case-sensitive language, which means that uppercase "A" and lowercase "a" are regarded as totally different items.

- **Termination** – All statements in C# language must be terminated by a **;** semicolon character, just as all sentences in English language must be terminated by a **.** period character. For example: **Console.WriteLine(** "Hello World!" **) ;**

- **Single-line comments** – Brief comments on a single line must begin with **//** two forward slash characters. For example: **// Output the traditional greeting.**

- **Block comments** – Extended comments on multiple lines must begin with **/*** forward slash and asterisk characters, and must end with the reverse ***/** asterisk and forward slash. For example:
  /*
  C# Programming in easy steps.
  Getting started with the traditional greeting.
  */

- **White space** – Spaces, tabs, newline characters, and comments are ignored by the C# compiler, so can be used extensively to organize code without performance penalty.

- **Escape sequences** – The C# compiler recognizes **\n** as a newline character and **\t** as a tab character, so these can be used to format output. For example: **Console.WriteLine(**"Line One \n Line Two"**) ;**

- **Naming conventions** – A programmer-defined identifier name in C# code may begin with an **_** underscore character or a letter in uppercase or lowercase. The name may also contain an underscore, letters, and numerals. For example: **class MyNo1_Class**

- **Keywords** – The C# language has a number of keywords (listed opposite) that have special syntactic meaning and may not be used to name programmer-defined items in code.

It is recommended that you comment your code to make it readily understood by others or when revisiting your own code later.

The **WriteLine( )** method automatically adds a newline after its output.

C# Reserved Keywords

abstract	as	base	bool
break	byte	case	catch
char	checked	class	const
continue	decimal	default	delegate
do	double	else	enum
event	explicit	extern	false
finally	fixed	float	for
foreach	goto	if	implicit
in	int	interface	internal
is	lock	long	namespace
new	null	object	operator
out	override	params	private
protected	public	readonly	ref
return	sbyte	sealed	short
sizeof	stackalloc	static	string
struct	switch	this	throw
true	try	typeof	uint
ulong	unchecked	unsafe	ushort
using	virtual	void	volatile
while			

Hot tip

If you absolutely must use a keyword to name a programmer-defined element, it may be prefixed by an @ character to distinguish it from the keyword – but this is best avoided.

C# Contextual Keywords

add	alias	ascending	async
await	descending	dynamic	from
get	global	group	into
join	let	orderby	partial
remove	select	set	value
var	where	yield	

Don't forget

Contextual keywords have special significance in certain code. For example, **get** and **set** in method declarations.

Summary

- **C#** is an object-oriented programming language that utilizes the proven functionality of the Microsoft **.NET** class libraries.
- The C# compiler generates **Intermediate Language (IL)** code that is stored on disk alongside resources in an assembly.
- The **Common Language Runtime (CLR)** examines an assembly's security requirements before JIT compilation.
- **Just-In-Time** compilation translates IL code into native machine code for execution by the operating system.
- Microsoft Visual Studio provides a fully **Integrated Development Environment (IDE)** for C# programming.
- A new Visual C# **Console** application generates default skeleton project code in the Visual Studio Code Editor.
- The Visual Studio **Solution Explorer** shows all files in a project, and the **Properties** window shows their properties.
- C# code needs to be added to the default skeleton code in the **Code Editor** to create a C# program.
- The **using System** directive allows the **System.Console** class to be written in the code without its **System.** prefix.
- The **Console** class has a **WriteLine( )** method that can be used to output a specified text string, and a **ReadKey( )** method that can recognize when the user presses any key.
- A C# program can be run in the Visual Studio IDE by selecting the **Debug**, **Start Debugging** menu, or by clicking the **Start** button, or by pressing the **F5** key.
- C# is a case-sensitive programming language in which all statements must be terminated by a ; semicolon character.
- Single-line // comments and /* */ block comments can be incorporated to explain C# program code.
- C# has keywords that have special syntactic meaning, so cannot be used to name programmer-defined code items.

2 Storing values

This chapter demonstrates how to store various types of data within a C# program.

Creating variables

A "variable" is like a container in a C# program in which a data value can be stored inside the computer's memory. The stored value can be referenced using the variable's name.

The programmer can choose any name for a variable, providing it adheres to the C# naming conventions – a chosen name may only contain letters, digits, and the underscore character, but must begin with a letter, underscore, or @ character. Also, the C# keywords must be avoided. It's good practice to choose meaningful names to make the code more comprehensible.

To create a new variable in a program it must be "declared", specifying the type of data it may contain and its chosen name. A variable declaration has this syntax:

data-type variable-name ;

Multiple variables of the same data type can be created in a single declaration as a comma-separated list with this syntax:

data-type variable-name1 , variable-name2 , variable-name3 ;

The most common C# data types are listed in the table below, together with a brief description and example content:

Data Type	Description
int	An integer whole number, e.g. **100**
char	A single character, e.g. **'A'**
float	A floating-point number of 7-digit precision
double	A floating-point number of 15-digit precision
decimal	A floating-point number of 28-digit precision
bool	A Boolean value of **true** or **false**
string	A string of characters, e.g. **"In Easy Steps"**

Variable declarations must appear before executable statements – so they will be available for reference within statements.

Names are case-sensitive in C# – so variables named **num**, **Num**, and **NUM** are treated as three individual variables. Traditionally, C# variable names are created in all lowercase characters.

Character values of the **char** data type must be enclosed in single quotes, but character strings of the **string** data type must be enclosed between double quotes.

The **decimal** data type is preferred for storage of monetary values.

When a value is assigned to a variable it is said to have been "initialized". Optionally, a variable may be initialized in its declaration. The value stored in any initialized variable can be displayed using the **WriteLine( )** method, which was used on page 16 to display the "Hello World!" greeting:

1 Open the Visual Studio IDE, then start a new **Console Application** project and name it "Variables"

2 Position the cursor between the **{ }** curly brackets of the **Main( )** method, then type this code to name the Console
```
Console.Title = "Variables" ;
```

3 Next, precisely type these statements to declare and initialize variables of common C# data types
```
char letter ;        letter = 'A' ;       // Declared then initialized.
int number ;         number = 100 ;  // Declared then initialized.
float body = 98.6f ;              // Declared and initialized.
double pi = 3.14159 ;             // Declared and initialized.
decimal sum = 1000.00m ;          // Declared and initialized.
bool flag = false ;               // Declared and initialized.
string text = "C# Is Fun" ;       // Declared and initialized.
```

4 Now, insert statements to display each stored value
```
Console.WriteLine( "char letter:\t" + letter ) ;
Console.WriteLine( "int number:\t" + number ) ;
Console.WriteLine( "float body:\t" + body ) ;
Console.WriteLine( "double pi:\t" + pi ) ;
Console.WriteLine( "decimal sum:\t" + sum ) ;
Console.WriteLine( "bool flag:\t" + flag ) ;
Console.WriteLine( "string text:\t" + text ) ;
Console.ReadKey( ) ;
```

5 Press **Start** to run the application and see the stored values

```
C:\ Variables                              —   □   ×
char letter:    A
int number:     100
float body:     98.6
double pi:      3.14159
decimal sum:    1000.00
bool flag:      False
string text:    C# Is Fun
```

Variables

Suffix **f** to a **float** value and **m** to a **decimal** value to distinguish them from a **double** value.

23

The inclusion of \t in the string is an "escape sequence" that prints a tab in the output. The + symbol is a "concatenation" operator, which adds the stored value to the string for output.

Reading input

In order to interact with the user, C# programs will typically require the user to input some values. The **ReadLine( )** method – a companion to the **ReadKey( )** method – can be used to read user input. User input within the Console can be assigned to a **string** variable by the **ReadLine( )** method when the user hits **Enter** to complete a line.

When requesting user input, it's preferable to prompt the user without adding a newline after the request. This is easily achieved using the Console.**Write( )** method:

Beware

It is important to recognize that the **ReadLine( )** method always reads input as a **string** value.

Input

Hot tip

Notice how two **+** concatenation operators are used here to insert input into a string.

1. Open the Visual Studio IDE, then start a new **Console Application** project and name it "Input"

2. Position the cursor between the **{ }** curly brackets of the **Main( )** method, then type this code to name the Console
   Console.**Title = "Input" ;**

3. Next, precisely type these statements to request user input for assignment to a variable
   Console.**Write("Please Enter Your Name: ") ;**
   string name = Console.**ReadLine( ) ;**

4. Now, add statements to display a message containing the stored user input value
   Console.**WriteLine("Welcome " + name + "!") ;**
   Console.**ReadKey( ) ;**

5. Press **Start** or **F5** to run the application and see the stored user input value displayed in output

```
Input                                    —    □    ×
Please Enter Your Name: Mike McGrath
Welcome Mike McGrath!
```

Numerical values input by the user are assigned to the **string** variable as characters – so arithmetic cannot be performed on these.

When you require the user to input numerical values it is necessary to convert the **string** values read by the **ReadLine( )** method into numerical data types. The **System**.Convert class provides a number of useful methods for this purpose, including:

Method	Returns
Convert.**ToInt32( )**	A 32-bit signed integer
Convert.**ToDouble( )**	A floating-point precision number
Convert.**ToDecimal( )**	A decimal precision number

Hot tip

There is also a useful Convert.**ToString( )** method to translate values to **string** type.

The **string** value read by the **ReadLine( )** method needs simply to be specified within the parentheses of the appropriate method:

1 Start a new **Console Application**, then name the project and Console.**Title** as "Conversion"

Conversion

2 Type these statements to request user input for conversion and assignment to two variables
```
Console.Write( "Please Enter A Number: " ) ;
double num = Convert.ToDouble( Console.ReadLine( ) ) ;
Console.Write( "Now Enter Another Number: " ) ;
double sum=
        num + Convert.ToDouble( Console.ReadLine( ) ) ;
```

3 Now, add statements to display a message containing the sum total of the user input values
```
Console.WriteLine( "Total = " + sum ) ;
Console.ReadKey( ) ;
```

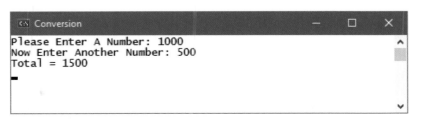

Don't forget

Here, the second input number gets converted to a numerical value before addition to the first input number.

4 Press **Start** or **F5** to run the application, then enter two values to see the converted input added in output

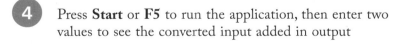

```
Conversion                                    —    □    ×
Please Enter A Number: 1000
Now Enter Another Number: 500
Total = 1500
```

Employing arrays

An array is a variable that can store multiple items of data – unlike a regular variable, which can only store one piece of data. The pieces of data are stored sequentially in array "elements" that are numbered, starting at zero. So, the first value is stored in element zero, the second value is stored in element one, and so on.

An array is declared by stating the data type, suffixed by [ ] square brackets to denote an array. This alone does not initialize the array variable in memory until an array "instance" is created by specifying an element size using the **new** keyword, like this:

data-type [ ] *array-name* = new *data-type*[*size*] ;

Values can then be individually assigned to each available element:

array-name[*element-number*] = *value* ;

Alternatively, an array can be initialized and values assigned to each element when it is declared by stating values for each element in a comma-separated list, grouped within braces:

data-type [ ] *array-name* =
      new *data-type*[*size*] { *value* , *value* , *value* } ;

Any individual element's value can be referenced using the array name followed by square brackets containing the element number – for example, to reference the value within the first element:

array-name[0]

Collectively, the elements of an array are known as an "index". Arrays can have more than one index – to represent multiple dimensions, rather than the single dimension of a regular array. Multi-dimensional arrays of three indices and more are uncommon, but two-dimensional arrays are useful to store grid-based information such as coordinates.

To create a multi-dimensional array, the [ ] square brackets following the data type in the declaration must contain a comma for each additional index. Similarly, the size of each index must be specified as a comma-separated list, like this:

data-type [,] *array-name* = new *data-type*[*size* , *size*] ;

Values can then be individually assigned to each available element:

array-name[*element-number* , *element-number*] = *value* ;

Array numbering starts at zero – so the final element in an array of six elements is number five, not number six. This numbering is known as a "zero-based index".

26

You can only store data within array elements of the data type specified in the array declaration.

A special **foreach** loop construct allows you to easily iterate through all elements of an array – see page 56 for details.

...cont'd

Alternatively, a multi-dimensional array can be initialized and values assigned to each element when it is declared by stating values for each index in a comma-separated list, grouped within braces – in a comma-separated group enclosed within braces:

data-type [,] *array-name* = new *data-type*[*size*]
    { { *value* , *value* , *value* } , { *value* , *value* , *value* } } ;

Any individual element's value can be referenced using the array name followed by square brackets containing the element number for each index. For example, to reference the value within the first element of the second index:

array-name[1 , 0]

The number of specified values must exactly match the specified array size to avoid an error.

Arrays

1. Start a new **Console Application**, then name the project and Console.**Title** as "Arrays"

2. Next, type this statement to create a string array
   string [ ] cars = new string[3] { "BMW", "Ford", "Opel" **} ;**

3. Now, type this statement to create a 2-dimensional array
   int [,] coords = new int[2, 3] { { 1, 2, 3 } , { 4, 5, 6 } } ;

4. Add statements to display output containing the stored array element values
   Console.**WriteLine(** "Second Car: " + **cars[1]) ;**
   Console.**WriteLine(** "X1,Y1: " + **coords[0, 0]) ;**
   Console.**WriteLine(** "X2,Y3: " + **coords[1, 2]) ;**
   Console.**ReadKey( ) ;**

5. Press **Start** or **F5** to run the application and see the values stored within array elements

X ⟶
	[0]	[1]
[0]	1	4
[1]	2	5
[2]	3	6

Y

Casting is also known as "type conversion".

Don't forget

The result of dividing an integer by another integer is truncated, not rounded – so a result of 9.9 would become 9.

Casting data types

A value stored in a variable can be forced (coerced) into a variable of a different data type by converting the value to a different type. This process is known as "casting", and may be implicit or explicit.

- **Implicit** casting is automatically performed by C# in a type-safe manner when converting numbers from smaller to larger precision data types, for example, when adding an **int** to a **double**.

- **Explicit** casting, on the other hand, requires a cast operator to be included in a statement to specify the data type to which the value should be cast. The required new data type must be specified in parentheses preceding the name of the variable containing the data to be cast, so its syntax looks like this:

variable-name = (*data-type*) *variable-name* ;

This is the traditional form of casting that is also found in the C programming language. Casting is often necessary to accurately store the result of an arithmetic operation to prevent data loss. Division of one integer by another integer will always produce an integer result, which may be truncated. For example, the integer division **7/2** produces the truncated integer result of **3**.

To store the accurate floating-point result would require the result be cast into a suitable data type, such as a **double**, like this:

double sum = (double) 7 / 2 ;   // Sum is 3.5

It should be noted that operator precedence casts the first operand **7** into the specified data type before implementing the arithmetic operation **/2** division, so effectively the statement is:

double sum = (double) (7) / 2 ;   // Sum is 3.5

Bracketing the expression as **(7 / 2)** would perform the arithmetic first on integers, so the integer result would be truncated before being cast into the **float** variable – not the desired effect!

double sum = (double) (7 / 2) ;   // Sum is 3.0

Single character values can usefully be explicitly cast to an **int** data type to reveal their ASCII code value. Similarly, the process can be reversed to reveal the character value of an integer.

1 Start a new **Console Application**, then name the project and Console.**Title** as "Cast"

Cast

2 Type these statements to create and initialize an integer variable and a double-precision floating-point variable
```
double num = 10.5 ;
int integer = 2 ;
```

3 Next, add statements to implicitly cast the integer value into a double-precision value, and display the result
```
num = num + integer ;
Console.WriteLine( "Implicit Cast: " + num ) ;
```

4 Now, explicitly cast the result of an integer division into a double-precision value, and display that result
```
num = ( double ) 7 / integer ;
Console.WriteLine( "Explicit Cast: " + num ) ;
```

Hot tip

Remove the **(double)** cast from Step 4 to see the result become truncated.

5 Cast an integer value into a **char** data type and display its ASCII equivalent character
```
char letter = ( char ) 65 ;
Console.WriteLine( "Cast Integer: " + letter ) ;
```

6 Cast a character value into an **int** data type and display its ASCII equivalent code number
```
int ascii = ( int ) 'A' ;
Console.WriteLine( "Cast Letter: " + ascii ) ;
Console.ReadKey( ) ;
```

Hot tip

ASCII (pronounced "askee") is the American Standard Code for Information Interchange, which is the accepted standard for plain text. In ASCII, characters are represented numerically within the range 0-127. Uppercase 'A' is 65 so that integer value gets cast into an **int** variable.

7 Press **Start** or **F5** to run the application and see the values cast into other data types

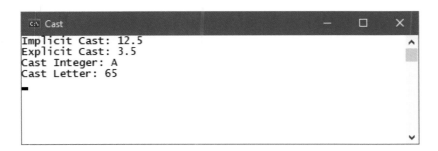

```
Cast                                    —    □    ×
Implicit Cast: 12.5
Explicit Cast: 3.5
Cast Integer: A
Cast Letter: 65
```

29

Declaring variables using the **var** keyword can make the program code less readable, as it does not indicate data types.

Don't forget

An enumerator list cannot be declared within any method block, so must be declared outside the **Main( )** method.

Fixing constants

Variable declarations explicitly specify their permissible data type using keywords such as **string, int,** or **double** to ensure the program cannot accidentally assign inappropriate data. Where you are certain this will never occur, you may use the **var** (variant) keyword when declaring a variable, to implicitly specify its data type according to the data type of its initial value. In this case, the C# compiler will automatically determine the appropriate data type. The **var** keyword is most useful to store a value that is other than of the standard C# numerical, Boolean, or string data types. All variable declarations made using the **var** keyword must assign an initial value to immediately determine that variable's data type.

The data type of any variable can be revealed by dot-suffixing the **GetType( )** method onto the variable name. For example, where a **num** variable is a **double** data type, calling **num.GetType( )** will return a **System.Double** result.

When a stored value is never intended to be changed, a "constant" container can be created to safeguard it from change. Its declaration is similar to that of a variable, but begins with the **const** keyword. Each declaration made using the **const** keyword must assign an initial value to immediately fix its constant value.

Multiple constant values can be defined in an enumerator list using the **enum** keyword and a specified identifier name. This creates a data type that consists of a comma-separated list of named constants within **{ }** braces. The enumerator list has an underlying default **int** value that numbers the list names from zero, much like the elements in an array. Any name within the list can be referenced by dot-suffixing it to the list name, and its underlying value revealed by casting.

The C# **Enum** class provides several methods to work with enumerator lists. Many of these require the data type of the list as an argument, so this can usefully be assigned to a **var** variable by specifying the list name as an argument to the **typeof( )** method. The **Enum** class **GetName( )** method can reveal the name at a specified index position, and the **IsDefined( )** method can be used to test whether the list contains a specified name. An enumerator list declaration must be written directly within the program namespace or within a class block.

1 Start a new **Console Application**, then name the project and Console.**Title** as "Constant"

Constant

2 Type this statement within the **class** block, before the **Main( )** method block, to create an enumerator list
enum Days **{ Sat, Sun, Mon, Tue, Wed, Thu, Fri } ;**

3 Now, turn your attention to the **Main( )** method, then declare and initialize a constant and a variable
const double pi = 3.14159265358979 ;
var daysType = typeof(Days **) ;**

4 Next, add statements to reveal the constant's data type and use its value for output
Console.**WriteLine(** "Pi Type: " **+ pi.GetType( )) ;**
Console.**WriteLine(** "Circumference: " **+ (pi * 3)) ;**

5 Then, add statements to display the name and index position of the first item in the enumerator list
Console.**WriteLine(** "\nFirst Name: " **+** Days.**Sat) ;**
Console.**WriteLine(** "1st Index: " **+ (int)** Days.**Sat) ;**

6 Finally, add statements to display the name at the second index position and to query the enumerator list
string name = Enum.**GetName(** daysType **, 1) ;**
Console.**WriteLine(** "\n2nd Index: " **+ name) ;**
bool flag = Enum.**IsDefined(** daysType **, "Mon") ;**
Console.**WriteLine(** "Contains Mon?: " **+ flag) ;**
Console.**ReadKey( ) ;**

7 Press **Start** or **F5** to run the application and see the constant values in operation

```
C:\ Constant                              —    □    ×
Pi Type: System.Double
Circumference: 9.42477796076937

First Name: Sat
1st Index: 0

2nd Index: Sun
Contains Mon?: True
```

The enumerator list contains names, not strings, so they need not be enclosed in quote marks, but the name must be supplied as a string argument to the **IsDefined( )** method.

You may want to avoid the **var** keyword where possible to be sure of variable data types. For example, with the line
var id = getID( ) ;
the assigned value (and therefore the variable data type) could be numeric or a string.

Summary

- A variable stores a data value within the computer's memory, and the value can be referenced using that variable's name.

- A variable declaration must specify the type of data it may contain, and a valid programmer-specified name.

- Common C# data types include **int, char, float, double, decimal, bool,** and **string**.

- Variables must be declared before they can be referenced.

- A variable becomes initialized when it is assigned a value.

- The Console.**ReadLine( )** method can be used to assign user input to a variable.

- The Console.**WriteLine( )** method adds a newline after its output, but the Console.**Write( )** method does not.

- The **System.**Convert class provides a number of useful methods to convert string values to numerical data types.

- An array variable can store multiple items of data within sequential elements of a zero-based index.

- An array declaration must specify the type of data it may contain, followed by [ ] and a programmer-specified name.

- An array is not initialized until an array instance is created using the **new** keyword to specify data type and element size.

- Values can be assigned to individual array elements using the array name and the element index number.

- An array declaration can assign values to all of its array elements as a comma-separated list of values within **{ }** braces.

- Arrays can have more than one index, to represent multiple dimensions where each index is separated by a comma.

- Casting is the conversion of one data type to another.

- Implicit casting is performed automatically by C#.

- Explicit casting is performed by including a cast operator within a statement, to specify the required new data type.

3 Performing operations

This chapter introduces C#
operators and demonstrates
the operations they can
perform.

The **%** modulus operator is also known as the "remainder" operator.

The **+** operator is dual-purpose – it is also used to concatenate strings.

Values used with operators to form expressions are called "operands" – in the expression **2 + 3** the numerical values **2** and **3** are the operands.

Doing arithmetic

The arithmetic operators commonly used in C# programs are listed in the table below, together with the operation they perform:

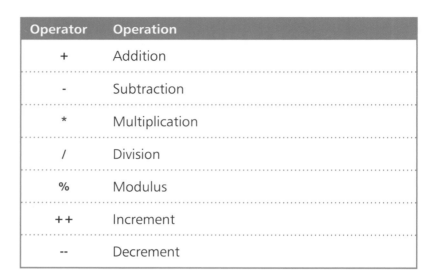

Operator	Operation
+	Addition
-	Subtraction
*	Multiplication
/	Division
%	Modulus
++	Increment
--	Decrement

The operators for assignment, addition, subtraction, multiplication, and division act as you would expect, but care must be taken to group expressions where more than one operator is used – operations within innermost **( )** parentheses are performed first:

```
a = b * c - d % e / f ;              // This is unclear.

a = ( b * c ) - ( ( d % e ) / f ) ;  // This is clearer.
```

The **%** modulus operator will divide the first given number by the second given number and return the remainder of the operation. This is useful to determine if a number has an odd or an even value.

The **++** increment operator and **--** decrement operator alter the given number by one and return the resulting value. These are most commonly used to count iterations in a loop – counting up on each iteration with the **++** increment operator, or counting down on each iteration with the **--** decrement operator.

The **++** increment and **--** decrement operators can be placed before or after a value to different effect – placed before the operand (prefix), its value is immediately changed; placed after the operand (postfix), its value is noted first, then the value is changed.

1 Start a new **Console Application**, then name the project and Console.**Title** as "Arithmetic"

Arithmetic

2 Type these statements to create and initialize two integer variables
```
int a = 8 ;
int b = 4 ;
```

3 Next, add statements to output the result of each basic arithmetical operation
```
Console.WriteLine( "Addition:\t: " + ( a + b ) ) ;
Console.WriteLine( "Subtraction:\t: " + ( a - b ) ) ;
Console.WriteLine( "Multiplication:\t: " + ( a * b ) ) ;
Console.WriteLine( "Division:\t: " + ( a / b ) ) ;
Console.WriteLine( "Modulus:\t: " + ( a % b ) ) ;
```

4 Now, add statements to output the result of a postfix increment operation
```
Console.WriteLine( "\nPostfix Increment:\t: " + ( a++ ) ) ;
Console.WriteLine( "Postfix Result.....:\t: " + a ) ;
```

Here, the \t escape sequence is used to output a tab space, and the \n escape sequence is used to output additional newlines.

5 Finally, add statements to output the result of a prefix increment operation – for comparison with postfix
```
Console.WriteLine( "\nPrefix Increment:\t: " + ( ++b ) ) ;
Console.WriteLine( "Prefix Result.....:\t: " + b ) ;
Console.ReadKey( ) ;
```

6 Press **Start** or **F5** to run the application and see the results produced by each arithmetic operator

```
c:\ Arithmetic                              —    □    ×
Addition:        12
Subtraction:     4
Multiplication:  32
Division:        2
Modulus:         0

Postfix Increment:      8
Postfix Result.....     9

Prefix Increment:       5
Prefix Result.....      5
```

Remember that a prefix operator changes the variable value <u>immediately</u> but a postfix operator changes the value <u>subsequently</u>.

Assigning values

The operators that are used in C# programming to assign values are listed in the table below. All except the simple = assignment operator are a shorthand form of a longer expression, so each equivalent is given for clarity:

Operator	Example	Equivalent
=	a = b	a = b
+=	a += b	a = (a + b)
-=	a -= b	a = (a - b)
*=	a *= b	a = (a * b)
/=	a /= b	a = (a / b)
%=	a %= b	a = (a % b)

The += combined operator is dual-purpose – it can also be used to concatenate strings.

It is important to regard the = operator to mean "assign" rather than "equals" to avoid confusion with the == equality operator that is described on page 38.

In the assignment example above, where **a = b**, the variable named "a" is assigned the value that is contained in the variable named "b" – so that is then the value stored in the **a** variable. Technically speaking, the assignment operator stores the value of the right-hand operand in the memory location denoted by the left-hand operand, then returns the value as a result.

The **+=** combined operator is useful to add a value onto an existing value that is stored in the **a** variable. In the example above, where **a += b**, the value in variable **b** is added to that in variable **a** – so the total is then the value stored in the **a** variable. The arithmetic operation is performed first with the grouped operands. The result is then stored in the memory location denoted by the first variable and returned.

All the other combined operators work in the same way by making the arithmetical operation between the two values first, then assigning the result of that operation to the first variable – to become its new stored value.

With the **%=** combined operator, the grouped left-hand operand **a** is divided by the grouped right-hand operand **b**, then the remainder of that operation is assigned to the **a** first variable.

...cont'd

Assign

1 Start a new **Console Application**, then name the project and Console.**Title** as "Assign"

2 Type these statements to declare two integer variables
```
int a ;
int b ;
```

3 Next, add statements to output simple assigned values
```
Console.Write( "Assign Values: " ) ;
Console.Write( "\t a = " + ( a = 8 ) ) ;
Console.WriteLine( "\t b = " + ( b = 4 ) ) ;
```

4 Now, add statements to output combined assigned values
```
Console.Write( "\n\nAdd and Assign: " ) ;
Console.Write( "\t a += b (8 += 4)\t a = " + ( a += b ) ) ;

Console.Write( "\n\nSubtract and Assign: " ) ;
Console.Write( "\t a -= b (12 -= 4)\t a = " + ( a -= b ) ) ;

Console.Write( "\n\nMultiply and Assign: " ) ;
Console.Write( "\t a *= b (8 *= 4)\t a = " + ( a *= b ) ) ;

Console.Write( "\n\nDivide and Assign: " ) ;
Console.Write( "\t a /= b (32 /= 4)\t a = " + ( a /= b ) ) ;

Console.Write( "\n\nModulus and Assign: " ) ;
Console.Write( "\t a %= b (8 %= 4)\t a = " + ( a %= b ) ) ;
Console.ReadKey( ) ;
```

Hot tip

Notice how \n\n escape sequences are used here to add two newlines for spacing output.

5 Press **Start** or **F5** to run the application and see the results produced by each assignment operator

```
C# Assign                                        —   □   ×
Assign Values:     a = 8    b = 4
Add and Assign:          a += b (8 += 4)        a = 12
Subtract and Assign:     a -= b (12 -= 4)       a = 8
Multiply and Assign:     a *= b (8 *= 4)        a = 32
Divide and Assign:       a /= b (32 /= 4)       a = 8
Modulus and Assign:      a %= b (8 %= 4)        a = 0_
```

Beware

The operands must be of the same data type, or the right-hand operand must be implicitly convertible to the type of the left-hand operand.

Comparing values

The operators that are commonly used in C# programming to compare two numerical values are listed in the table below:

The comparison operators are also known as "relational operators".

Operator	Comparative test
==	Equality
!=	Inequality
>	Greater than
<	Less than
>=	Greater than or equal to
<=	Less than or equal to

You can specify a Boolean value to the **Convert.ToDouble()** method to discover that **true** is represented numerically as 1, and **false** is represented as 0.

The == equality operator compares two operands and will return **true** if both are equal in value, otherwise the == operator will return **false**. If both are the same number, they are equal, or if both are characters, their ASCII code values are compared numerically.

Conversely, the != inequality operator returns **true** if two operands are not equal, using the same rules as the == equality operator, otherwise it returns **false**. Equality and inequality operators are useful in testing the state of two variables to perform conditional branching in a program.

The > "greater than" operator compares two operands and will return **true** if the first is greater in value than the second, or it will return **false** if it is equal or less in value. The < "less than" operator makes the same comparison but returns **true** if the first operand is less in value than the second, otherwise it returns **false**. Typically, a > "greater than" or < "less than" operator is used to test the value of an iteration counter in a loop structure.

Adding the = assignment operator after a > "greater than" operator or a < "less than" operator makes it also return **true** if the two operands are exactly equal in value.

1 Start a new **Console Application**, then name the project and Console.**Title** as "Comparison"

Comparison

2 Type these statements to declare three integer variables and two character variables to be compared
```
int nil = 0 , num = 0 , max = 1 ;
char cap = 'A' , low = 'a' ;
```

3 Next, add statements to output the result of equality comparisons of integers and characters
```
Console.Write( "Equality:" ) ;
Console.Write( "\t (0 == 0) : " + ( nil == num ) ) ;
Console.Write( "\n\t\t (A == a) : " + ( cap == low ) ) ;
```

The ASCII code value for uppercase '**A**' is 65 but for lowercase '**a**' it's 97 – so their comparison here returns **false**.

4 Now, add statements to output the result of other integer comparisons
```
Console.Write( "\n\nInequality:" ) ;
Console.Write( "\t (0 != 1) : " + ( nil != max ) ) ;

Console.Write( "\n\nGreater:" ) ;
Console.Write( "\t (0 > 1) : " + ( nil > max ) ) ;

Console.Write( "\nLess:" ) ;
Console.Write( "\t\t (0 < 1) : " + ( nil < max ) ) ;

Console.Write( "\n\nGreater/Equal:" ) ;
Console.Write( "\t (0 >= 0) : " + ( nil >= num ) ) ;

Console.Write( "\nLess or Equal:" ) ;
Console.Write( "\t (1 <= 0) : " + ( max <= nil ) ) ;
Console.ReadKey( ) ;
```

When comparing numbers, remember to test for equality as well as testing for higher and lower values.

5 Press **Start** or **F5** to run the application and see the results produced by each comparison

```
C# Comparison                                    —    □    ×
Equality:        (0 == 0) : True
                 (A == a) : False

Inequality:      (0 != 1) : True

Greater:         (0 > 1) : False
Less:            (0 < 1) : True

Greater/Equal:   (0 >= 0) : True
Less or Equal:   (1 <= 0) : False
```

Assessing logic

The logical operators most commonly used in C# programming are listed in the table below:

Operator	Operation
&&	Logical-AND
||	Logical-OR
!	Logical-NOT

The logical operators are used with operands that have Boolean values of **true** or **false**, or are values that convert to **true** or **false**.

The **&&** logical-AND operator will evaluate two operands and return **true** only if both operands themselves are **true**. Otherwise, the **&&** logical-AND operator will return **false**. This is used in conditional branching where the direction of a program is determined by testing two conditions – if both conditions are satisfied, the program will go in a certain direction, otherwise it will take a different direction.

Unlike the **&&** logical-AND operator, which needs both operands to be **true**, the **||** logical-OR operator will evaluate its two operands and return **true** if either one of the operands itself returns **true**. If, however, neither operand returns **true**, then the **||** logical-OR operator will return **false**. This is useful in C# programming to perform a certain action if either one of two test conditions has been met.

The **!** logical-NOT operator is a unary operator that is used before a single operand. It returns the inverse value of the given operand, so if the variable **a** had a value of **true** then **!a** would have a value of **false**. The **!** logical-NOT operator is useful in C# programs to toggle the value of a variable in successive loop iterations with a statement like **a = !a**. This ensures that on each pass the value is changed, like flicking a light switch on and off.

Hot tip

The term "Boolean" refers to a system of logical thought developed by the English mathematician George Boole (1815-1864).

① Start a new **Console Application**, then name the project and Console.**Title** as "Logic"

Logic

② Type this statement to declare two Boolean variables
```
bool yes = true , no = false ;
```

③ Add these statements to output the result of AND logic
```
Console.Write( "AND Logic:" ) ;
Console.Write( "\t (yes && yes) : " + ( yes && yes ) ) ;
Console.Write( "\n\t\t (yes && no ) : " + ( yes && no ) ) ;
Console.Write( "\n\t\t (no  && no ) : " + ( no && no ) ) ;
```

④ Now, add statements to output the result of OR logic
```
Console.Write( "\n\nOR Logic:" ) ;
Console.Write( "\t (yes || yes) : " + ( yes || yes ) ) ;
Console.Write( "\n\t\t (yes || no ) : " + ( yes || no ) ) ;
Console.Write( "\n\t\t (no  || no ) : " + ( no || no ) ) ;
```

⑤ Then, add statements to output the result of NOT logic
```
Console.Write( "\n\nNOT Logic:" ) ;
Console.Write( "\t yes = " + yes ) ;
Console.Write( "\t !yes = " + !yes ) ;
Console.Write( "\n\t\t no = " + no ) ;
Console.Write( "\t !no = " + !no ) ;
Console.ReadKey( ) ;
```

The value returned by the ! logical-NOT operator is the inverse of the stored value – the stored value itself remains unchanged.

⑥ Press **Start** or **F5** to run the application and see the results produced by each logical operation

```
C:\ Logic                                            —    □    ×
AND Logic:      (yes && yes) : True                              ^
                (yes && no ) : False
                (no  && no ) : False

OR Logic:       (yes || yes) : True
                (yes || no ) : True
                (no  || no ) : False

NOT Logic:      yes = True       !yes = False
                no  = False      !no  = True

                                                                 v
```

Notice that **false && false** returns **false**, not **true** – demonstrating the maxim "two wrongs don't make a right".

Examining conditions

Possibly, the C# programmer's favorite test operator is the **?:** "ternary" operator. This operator first evaluates an expression for a **true** or **false** condition, then returns one of two specified values depending on the result of the evaluation. For this reason it is also known as the "conditional" operator.

The **?:** ternary operator has this syntax:

(*test-expression*) ? *if-true-return-this* : *if-false-return-this* ;

The ternary operator has three operands – the one before the **?** and those before and after the **:**.

Although the ternary operator can initially appear a little confusing, it is well worth becoming familiar with this operator as it can execute powerful program branching with minimal code – for example, to branch when a variable is not a value of one:

(*variable* != 1) ? *if-true-do-this* : *if-false-do-this* ;

The ternary operator is commonly used in C# programming to assign the maximum or minimum value of two variables to a third variable, for example, to assign a minimum, like this:

c = (a < b) ? a : b ;

The expression in parentheses returns **true** when the value of variable **a** is less than that of variable **b** – so in this case, the lesser value of variable **a** gets assigned to variable **c**.

Similarly, replacing the **<** less than operator in the test expression with the **>** greater than operator would assign the greater value of variable **b** to variable **c**.

Value equality, where two variables contain an equal value, is also known as "equivalence".

Another common use of the ternary operator incorporates the **%** modulus operator in the test expression to determine whether the parity value of a variable is an odd number or an even number:

(*variable* % 2 != 0) ? *if-true(odd)-do-this* : *if-false(even)-do-this* ;

Where the result of dividing the variable value by two does leave a remainder, the number is odd – where there is no remainder, the number is even. The test expression (*variable* % 2 == 1) would have the same effect, but it is preferable to test for inequality – it's easier to spot when something is different than when it's identical.

1 Start a new **Console Application**, then name the project and Console.**Title** as "Condition"

Condition

2 Type this statement to declare and initialize two integer variables
```
int a = 8 ;
int b = 3 ;
```

3 Next, add these statements to output an appropriate string with correct grammar for quantity
```
string verb = ( a != 1 ) ? " are " : " is " ;
Console.Write( "There" + verb + a +"\n" ) ;
```

4 Now, add statements to output an appropriate string correctly describing the parity of each variable value
```
string parity = ( a % 2 != 0 ) ? "Odd" : "Even" ;
Console.Write( a + " is " + parity ) ;

parity = ( b % 2 != 0 ) ? "Odd" : "Even" ;
Console.Write( b + " is " + parity ) ;
```

5. Then, add statements to output a string reporting the greater of these two variable values
```
int max = ( a > b ) ? a : b ;
Console.Write( "\nMaximum is " + max ) ;
Console.ReadKey( ) ;
```

Hot tip

The **?:** ternary operator can return values of any data type – numbers, strings, Booleans, etc.

6 Press **Start** or **F5** to run the application and see the results produced by examining each variable value

```
Condition                                          —    □    ×
There are 8

8 is Even
3 is Odd

Maximum is 8
```

Setting precedence

Operator precedence determines the order in which C# evaluates expressions. For example, the expression **1 + 5 * 3** evaluates to 16, not 18, because the ***** multiplication operator has a higher precedence than the **+** addition operator. Parentheses can be used to specify precedence, so that **(1 + 5) * 3** evaluates to 18.

When operators have equal precedence, their "associativity" determines how expressions are grouped. For example, the - subtraction operator is left-associative, grouping left-to-right (LTR), so **8 - 4 - 2** is grouped as **(8 - 4) - 2** and thus evaluates to 2. Other operators are right-associative, grouping right-to-left (RTL).

The table below lists common operators in order of precedence, with the highest-precedence ones at the top. Operators on the same line have equal precedence, so operator associativity determines how expressions are grouped and evaluated.

Don't forget

The ***** multiply operator is on a higher row than the **+** addition operator – so in the expression **a=1+5*3**, multiplication is completed first, before the addition.

Hot tip

There are also a number of "bitwise" operators, which are used to perform binary arithmetic. This is outside the scope of this book but there is a section devoted to binary arithmetic in our book **C Programming in easy steps**. Those operators perform in just the same way in C#.

Category	Operator	Associativity
Postfix	( ) [ ] . ++ --	LTR ☞
Unary Sign Prefix	! + - ++ --	☜ RTL
Multiplicative	* / %	LTR ☞
Additive	+ -	LTR ☞
Comparative	< <= > >=	LTR ☞
Equivalence	== !=	LTR ☞
Conditional	&&	LTR ☞
Conditional	||	LTR ☞
Conditional	?:	☜ RTL
Assignment	= += -= *= /= %=	☜ RTL
Comma	,	LTR ☞

1 Start a new **Console Application**, then name the project and Console.**Title** as "Precedence"

Precedence

2 Type this statement to declare an integer variable
```
int sum ;
```

3 Add these statements to initialize the variable with the result of an ungrouped expression and display that result
```
sum = 1 + 4 * 3 ;
Console.Write( "Default Order:\t\t" + sum ) ;
```

The * multiplication operator takes precedence over the + addition operator – so multiplication is performed first.

4 Next, add statements to assign the result of a grouped expression and display that result
```
sum = ( 1 + 4 ) * 3 ;
Console.Write( "Forced Order:\t\t" + sum ) ;
```

5 Add statements to assign the result of a new ungrouped expression and display that result
```
sum = 7 - 4 + 2 ;
Console.Write( "\nDefault Direction:\t" + sum ) ;
```

The - subtraction operator and the + addition operator have equal precedence but also have left-to-right associativity – so subtraction is performed first before addition.

6 Now, add statements to assign the result of the new grouped expression and display that result
```
sum = 7 - ( 4 + 2 ) ;
Console.Write( "\nForced Direction:\t" + sum ) ;
Console.ReadKey( ) ;
```

7 Press **Start** or **F5** to run the application and see the results produced by examining each variable value

```
Precedence                                    —    □    ×
Default Order:          13
Forced Order:           15

Default Direction:      5
Forced Direction:       1
```

It is best to clarify all expressions by adding parentheses to group operations.

45

Summary

- Arithmetic operators can form expressions with two operands for **+** addition, **-** subtraction, ***** multiplication, and **/** division.

- The **%** modulus arithmetic operator divides the first operand by its second operand, then returns the remainder.

- Care must be taken to group expressions within **( )** parentheses where more than one operator is used.

- The **++** increment and **--** decrement operators may be postfixed or prefixed to modify a single operand by one.

- The **=** assignment operator can be combined with an arithmetic operator to assign the result of an operation.

- Comparison operators can form expressions with two operands for **==** equality or for **!=** inequality.

- Comparison operators can form expressions with two operands for **>** greater or for **<** lesser value comparison.

- Equality can also be recognized in comparisons with the **>=** greater-or-equal and **<=** less-or-equal operators.

- The **&&** logical-AND operator evaluates two operands and will return **true** only if both operands are themselves **true**.

- The **||** logical-OR operator evaluates two operands and will return **true** if either of the two operands are themselves **true**.

- The **!** logical-NOT operator returns the inverse Boolean value of a single given operand.

- The **?:** ternary operator evaluates a given Boolean expression, then returns one of two operands depending on the result.

- Operator precedence determines the order in which expressions are evaluated.

- When operators have equal precedence, their associativity determines how expressions are grouped for evaluation.

4 Making statements

Branching with if

The C# **if** keyword performs the basic conditional test that evaluates a given expression for a Boolean value of **true** or **false** – and its syntax looks like this:

if (*test-expression*) { *statements-to-execute-when-true* }

The braces following the test may contain one or more statements, each terminated by a ; semicolon, but these will only be executed when the expression is found to be **true**. When the test is found to be **false**, the program proceeds to its next task.

To allow "conditional branching", an **if** statement can offer alternative statements to execute when the test fails by appending an **else** statement block after the **if** statement block, like this:

if (*test-expression*) { *statements-to-execute-when-true* }
else { *statements-to-execute-when-false* }

To test two conditions, the test expression may use the **&&** operator. For example, if ((num > 5) && (letter == 'A')).

Alternatively, an **if** statement can be "nested" within another **if** statement, so those statements in the inner statement block will only be executed when both tests succeed – but statements in the outer statement block will be executed if the outer test succeeds:

Hot tip

Shorthand can be used when testing a Boolean value – so the expression **if(flag == true)** can be written as **if(flag)**.

Beware

Avoid nesting more than three levels of if statements – to prevent confusion and errors.

IfElse

1 Start a new **Console Application**, then name the project and Console.**Title** as "IfElse"

2 Type these statements to create and initialize two variables from user input
```
Console.Write( "Please Enter A Number: " ) ;
double num = Convert.ToDouble( Console.ReadLine( ) ) ;
Console.Write( "Thanks. Now Enter A Letter: " ) ;
char letter = Convert.ToChar( Console.ReadLine( ) ) ;
```

3 Next, add a statement to output a message if the user's number input exceeds a specified value
```
if ( num >= 6 )
{
  Console.WriteLine( "\nNumber Exceeds 5" ) ;
  // Nested statement to be inserted here (Step 5).
}
```

4 Now, add a statement to output an alternative message if the user's number input is less than the specified value

```
else
{
  Console.WriteLine( "\nNumber Is 5 Or Less" ) ;
}
Console.ReadKey( ) ;
```

5 Insert a statement within the if block to output a message when the user's letter input matches a specified value

```
if ( letter == 'C' )
{
  Console.WriteLine( "Letter Is 'C'" ) ;
}
```

6 Press **Start** or **F5** to run the application and enter values to see the program branch according to your input

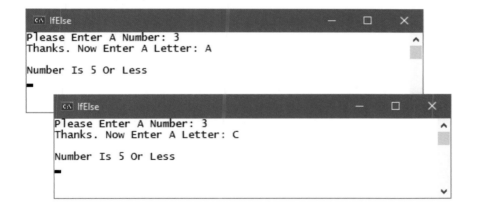

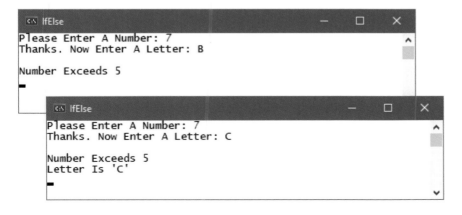

Switching branches

The **if** and **else** keywords, introduced on pages 48-49, allow programs to branch in a particular direction according to the result of a test condition, and can be used to repeatedly test a variable to match a value – for example, testing for an integer:

```
if ( num == 1 ) { Console.Write( "Monday" ) ; }
else
if ( num == 2 ) { Console.Write( "Tuesday" ) ; }
else
if ( num == 3 ) { Console.Write( "Wednesday" ) ; }
else
if ( num == 4 ) { Console.Write( "Thursday" ) ; }
else
if ( num == 5 ) { Console.Write( "Friday" ) ; }
```

The program will branch in the direction of the match.

Conditional branching with long **if-else** statements can often be more efficiently performed using a **switch** statement instead, especially when the test expression evaluates just one variable.

The **switch** statement works in an unusual way. It takes a given variable value, or expression, then seeks a matching value among a number of **case** statements. Statements associated with the matching **case** statement by a : colon will then be executed.

When no match is found, no **case** statements will be executed, but you may add a **default** statement after the final **case** statement to specify statements to be executed when no match is found. The syntax of a typical switch statement looks like this:

```
switch( variable-name )
{
  case value1 : statement ; break ;
  case value2 : statement ; break ;
  case value3 : statement ; break ;
  default : statement ; break ;
}
```

It is important to follow each case statement with the **break** keyword. Unlike other programming languages, C# does not allow fall-through from one **case** statement to another – each **case** statement must allow control to be handed back in order to exit the **switch** block.

Avoid writing lengthy **if-else** statements like the one shown here – where possible, use a **switch** statement instead.

Missing **break** keywords in C# **case** statements are syntax errors.

50

Switch

1 Start a new **Console Application**, then name the project and Console.**Title** as "Switch"

2 Type this statement to create and initialize an integer variable
int **num** = **3** ;

3 Next, add a statement to declare a **string** variable
string **day** ;

4 Now, add a statement to initialize the **string** variable according to the value of the integer variable
```
switch( num )
{
  case 1 : day = "Monday" ; break ;
  case 2 : day = "Tuesday" ; break ;
  case 3 : day = "Wednesday" ; break ;
  case 4 : day = "Thursday" ; break ;
  case 5 : day = "Friday" ; break ;
  // Default statement to be inserted here (Step 5).
}
```

A **case** statement can also try to match against a **string** value – for example: **case : "ABC"**.

51

5 Then, insert a final statement into the **switch** block to initialize the **string** variable when no match is found
default : **day** = "Weekend Day" ; break ;

6 Finally, add statements to output the assigned value
Console.**WriteLine**("Day " + **num** + " : " + **day**) ;
Console.**ReadKey**( ) ;

7 Press **Start** or **F5** to run the application and see the **string** result of the **switch** block assignment

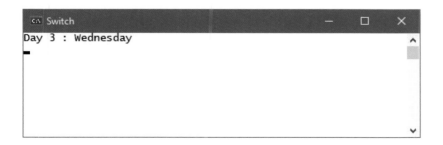

```
Switch                                    —    □    ×
Day 3 : Wednesday
```

Looping for

A loop is a piece of code in a program that automatically repeats. One complete execution of all statements contained within the loop block is known as an "iteration" or "pass".

The number of iterations made by a loop is controlled by a conditional test made within the loop. While the tested expression remains **true**, the loop will continue – until the tested expression becomes **false**, at which time the loop ends.

The three types of loop structures in C# programming are **for** loops, **while** loops, and **do-while** loops. Perhaps the most commonly used loop is the **for** loop, which has this syntax:

for (*initializer* ; *test-expression* ; *updater*) { *statements* }

The initializer sets the starting value for a counter of the number of iterations to be made by the loop. An integer variable is used for this purpose and is traditionally named "i".

Upon each iteration of the loop, the test expression is evaluated, and that iteration will only continue while this expression is **true**. When the tested expression becomes **false**, the loop ends immediately without executing the statements again. On each iteration, the counter is updated then the statements executed.

Hot tip

The updater may increment the counter using the **++** operator to count up, or decrement the counter using the **--** decrement operator to count down.

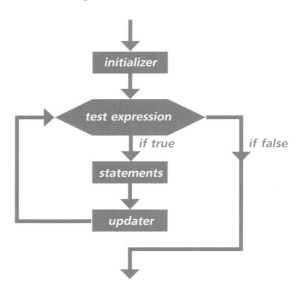

Loops may be nested within other loops – so that the inner loop will fully execute its iterations on each iteration of the outer loop.

...cont'd

ForLoop

1 Start a new **Console Application**, then name the project and Console.**Title** as "ForLoop"

2 Type these statements to create a loop that will make three iterations

```
for( int i = 1 ; i < 4 ; i++ )
{
  Console.WriteLine( "Loop Iteration: " + i ) ;
  // Nested loop to be inserted here (Step 4).
}
Console.ReadKey( ) ;
```

3 Press **Start** or **F5** to run the application and see the loop counter displayed on each iteration

```
cs ForLoop                                    —    □    ×
Loop Iteration: 1
Loop Iteration: 2
Loop Iteration: 3
```

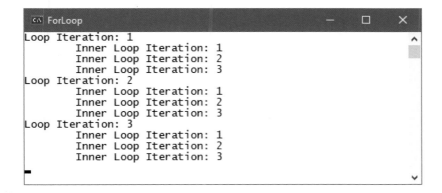

4 Inside the **for** loop block, insert another **for** loop that will also make three iterations

```
for( int j = 1 ; j < 4 ; j++ )
{
  Console.WriteLine( "\tInner Loop Iteration: " + j ) ;
}
```

5 Press **Start** or **F5** to run the application once more and now see both loop counters displayed on each iteration

```
cs ForLoop                                    —    □    ×
Loop Iteration: 1
        Inner Loop Iteration: 1
        Inner Loop Iteration: 2
        Inner Loop Iteration: 3
Loop Iteration: 2
        Inner Loop Iteration: 1
        Inner Loop Iteration: 2
        Inner Loop Iteration: 3
Loop Iteration: 3
        Inner Loop Iteration: 1
        Inner Loop Iteration: 2
        Inner Loop Iteration: 3
```

Don't forget

On the third iteration of these loops, the updater increments the counter value to **4** – so when it is next evaluated, the test expression returns **false** and the loop ends.

53

Looping while

An alternative to the **for** loop, introduced on pages 52-53, uses the **while** keyword, followed by an expression to be evaluated. When the expression is **true**, statements contained within braces following the test expression will be executed. The expression will then be evaluated again, and the **while** loop will continue until the expression is found to be **false**.

while (*test-expression*) { *statements* }

The loop's statement block <u>must</u> contain code that will affect the tested expression in order to change the evaluation result to **false**, otherwise an infinite loop is created that will lock the system! When the tested expression is found to be **false** upon its first evaluation, the **while** loop's statement block will never be executed.

A subtle variation of the **while** loop places the **do** keyword before the loop's statement block and a **while** test after it, with this syntax:

do { *statements* } while (*test-expression*) ;

In a **do-while** loop the statement block will always be executed at least once – because the expression is not evaluated until after the first iteration of the loop.

Breaking out of loops

A **break** statement can be included in any kind of loop to immediately terminate the loop when a test condition is met. The **break** ensures no further iterations of that loop will be executed.

Similarly, a **continue** statement can be included in any kind of loop to immediately terminate that particular iteration of the loop when a test condition is met. The **continue** statement allows the loop to proceed to the next iteration:

WhileLoop

1   Start a new **Console Application**, then name the project and Console.**Title** as "WhileLoop"

2   Type these statements to create and initialize an integer array variable and a regular integer counter variable
int [ ] nums = new int[10] ;
int i = 0 ;

3 Next, add a **while** loop to assign its incrementing counter value to an array element and display it on each iteration

```
while( i < nums.Length )
{
  nums[ i ] = i ;
  Console.Write( " | " + nums[ i ] ) ;
  i++ ;
}
Console.Write( "\n\n" ) ;
```

Notice how the array's **Length** property is used to determine the number of elements it contains.

4 Now, add a **do-while** loop to display its decrementing counter value on each iteration

```
do
{
  i-- ;
  // Statements to be inserted here (Step 6).
  Console.Write( " | " + nums[ i ] ) ;
}
while( i > 0 ) ;
Console.ReadKey( ) ;
```

Remember that the **while** statement at the end of a **do-while** loop must be terminated with a ; semicolon.

5 Press **Start** or **F5** to run the application and see both loop counters displayed on each iteration

```
C:\ WhileLoop                                    —    □    ×
| 0 | 1 | 2 | 3 | 4 | 5 | 6 | 7 | 8 | 9
| 9 | 8 | 7 | 6 | 5 | 4 | 3 | 2 | 1 | 0_
```

6 In the **do-while** loop, insert a statement to skip a single iteration, and a statement to prematurely exit the loop

```
if( i == 8 ) { Console.Write( " | Skipped" ) ; continue ; }
if( i == 3 ) { Console.Write( " | Done" ) ; break ; }
```

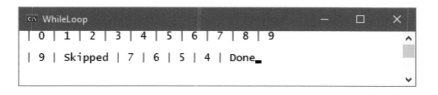

7 Press **Start** or **F5** to run the application once more, and now see the **do-while** loop iterations skipped

The position of **break** and **continue** statements is important – they must appear after the updater, to avoid creating an infinite loop, but before any other statements, to prevent their execution.

```
C:\ WhileLoop                                    —    □    ×
| 0 | 1 | 2 | 3 | 4 | 5 | 6 | 7 | 8 | 9
| 9 | Skipped | 7 | 6 | 5 | 4 | Done_
```

Use a **for** loop if you need to assign or modify element values.

ForEach

The **break** and **continue** keywords can be used in a **foreach** statement to exit the iteration cycle.

Iterating for each

C# provides a special **foreach-in** statement that allows you to easily traverse all elements in an array to access all stored values. This is an "iterator", rather than a loop structure, so it cannot be used to assign or modify element values – it can only be used to read their values. Syntax of a **foreach-in** statement looks like this:

foreach (*data-type variable-name* in *array-name*) { *statements* }

The **foreach** keyword must specify a variable of an appropriate data type to which each element value can be assigned, one by one, and the **in** keyword must specify the name of the array:

1 Start a new **Console Application**, then name the project and Console.**Title** as "ForEach"

2 Type this statement to create and initialize a **string** array
string [ ] websites = new string [5]
{ "Google", "YouTube", "Facebook", "Baidu", "Yahoo!" } ;

3 Next, add a statement to display a list heading
Console.**WriteLine(** "Popular Websites..." **) ;**

4 Now, add a **foreach** statement to display a counter value and element value on each iteration
int rank = 1 ;
foreach(string site in websites)
{
  Console.**WriteLine(** "Position: " + rank + "\t" + site **) ;**
  rank++ ;
}
Console.**ReadKey( ) ;**

5 Press **Start** or **F5** to run the application and see the iterator display the counter and element values

A **foreach-in** statement can also be used to traverse all elements of a C# "dictionary" that contains associated key-value pairs. The data types of the key and value must be specified as a comma-separated pair within < > angled brackets in the declaration:

```
Dictionary < data-type, data-type > dictionary-name =
        new Dictionary < data-type, data-type > ( ) ;
```

The **foreach** keyword must specify a KeyValuePair to which each key-value pair value can be assigned, one by one, and the **in** keyword must specify the name of the dictionary:

Beware

The Dictionary class is part of the **System. Collections.Generic** library – so this must be included in the program **using** statements.

KeyValue

1 Start a new **Console Application**, then name the project and Console.**Title** as "KeyValue"

2 Type these statements to create and initialize a dictionary named "BookList"
```
Dictionary < string, string > BookList =
        new Dictionary < string, string > ( ) ;
BookList.Add( "Stuart Yarnold", "Arduino" ) ;
BookList.Add( "Nick Vandome","Windows 10" ) ;
BookList.Add( "Mike McGrath", "Java" ) ;
```

3 Now, add a statement to display a list heading
```
Console.WriteLine( "Popular Titles..." ) ;
```

4 Add a **foreach** statement to display each key-value pair
```
foreach( KeyValuePair < string, string > book in BookList )
{
  Console.WriteLine( "Key: " + book.Key +
        "\tValue: "+ book.Value + " in easy steps" ) ;
}
Console.ReadKey( ) ;
```

5 Press **Start** or **F5** to run the application and see the iterator display the dictionary's key-value pairs

Hot tip

Note that a Dictionary object has **Add( )** and **Remove( )** methods, and has **Key** and **Value** properties.

```
CA KeyValue                                              —    □    ×
Popular Titles...
Key: Stuart Yarnold      Value: Arduino in easy steps
Key: Nick Vandome        Value: Windows 10 in easy steps
Key: Mike McGrath        Value: Java in easy steps
```

Summary

- An **if** statement evaluates a given test expression for a Boolean value of **true** or **false**.

- Statements contained in braces after an **if** statement will only be executed when the evaluation is found to be **true**.

- Multiple **if** statements can be nested, so statements in the inner loop are only executed when both loop tests return **true**.

- The **if** and **else** keywords are used to perform conditional branching according to the result of a tested expression.

- A **switch** statement is an alternative form of conditional branching that matches a **case** statement to a given value.

- Each **case** statement must be terminated by the **break** keyword, as C# does not allow fall-through.

- The **for** loop structure has parameters declaring an initializer, a test expression, and an updater.

- A loop updater may **++** increment a counter to count up, or may **--** decrement a counter to count down.

- A **while** loop may never execute its statements, but a **do-while** loop will always execute its statements at least once.

- A **while** loop and **do-while** loop must always have an updater within their loop body to avoid creating an infinite loop.

- Any type of loop can be immediately terminated by including a **break** statement within the loop body.

- A single iteration of any type of loop can be skipped by including a **continue** statement within the loop body.

- A **foreach-in** statement is an iterator that can traverse all elements of an array to read their values.

- A **foreach-in** statement can traverse all key-value pairs of a dictionary to read their values.

5 Devising methods

This chapter demonstrates how to create methods that can be called to execute statements whenever the C# program requires them.

Creating function

C# programmer-specified methods enclose a section of code that provides particular functionality to the program. When a method is called from within the default **Main( )** program method, its statements are executed and, optionally, a value can be returned to the main program upon completion. Wrapping functionality in modular methods provides these three main benefits:

● Modular program code is easier to understand and maintain.

● Tried and tested methods can be re-used by other programs.

● The workload on large programs can be more easily shared.

A method is declared in a C# program by specifying the various elements of its structure with this syntax:

access-specifier return-data-type method-name (parameters)
{
   statements
}

The access specifier determines the visibility of the method to other classes, using keywords such as **public** and **private**. Alternatively, if the method is not intended for use by other classes, it can be initialized in memory using the **static** keyword.

If the method will return a value to the caller, the data type of that value must be specified. If, on the other hand, the method will never return a value, the **void** keyword must be specified.

A name must be specified for each programmer-defined method, adhering to the same naming conventions as variable names.

Optionally, parameters may be specified within parentheses after the method name to represent argument values passed into the method by the caller. Once defined, a method without parameters may be called simply by stating its name followed by parentheses.

Variables declared within a method are not, by default, visible to other parts of the program – they are only available to code within that method body. The visibility of variables is known as "variable scope" and variables within methods have only "local" scope. This means that variables declared in different methods may be given the same name without conflict.

The first part of a method declaration, defining its access, return type, name, and parameters, is known as the method "signature".

The use of methods by other classes is described and demonstrated in the chapter on Object Oriented Programming – see page 112.

Parameters and arguments are demonstrated in the example on page 62.

C#

1. Start a new **Console Application**, then name the project and Console.**Title** as "Method"

2. After the **Main()** method, add this method definition within the **{ }** braces of the **class** Program
```
static void bodyTempC( )
{
  Console.WriteLine( "Body Temperature..." ) ;
  Console.WriteLine( "Centigrade:\t37°C" ) ;
}
```

Method

Hot tip

You can use the Windows Accessories, Character Map facility to produce the degree symbol.

3. Next, add a method definition that returns a floating-point value to the caller
```
static double bodyTempF( )
{
  double temperature = 98.6 ;
  return temperature ;
}
```

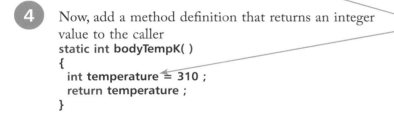

4. Now, add a method definition that returns an integer value to the caller
```
static int bodyTempK( )
{
  int temperature = 310 ;
  return temperature ;
}
```

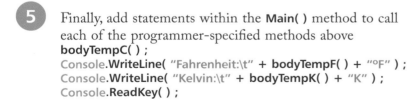

Don't forget

Each variable can share the same name as they have only local scope.

61

5. Finally, add statements within the **Main( )** method to call each of the programmer-specified methods above
```
bodyTempC( ) ;
Console.WriteLine( "Fahrenheit:\t" + bodyTempF( ) + "°F" ) ;
Console.WriteLine( "Kelvin:\t" + bodyTempK( ) + "K" ) ;
Console.ReadKey( ) ;
```

6. Press **Start** or **F5** to run the application and see the output featuring the method calls

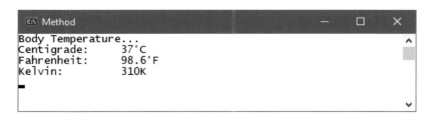

```
Method
Body Temperature...
Centigrade:     37°C
Fahrenheit:     98.6°F
Kelvin:         310K
```

Passing arguments

Methods may optionally specify one or more parameters as a comma-separated list within the parentheses of their definition. Each specified parameter must state the data type it may contain, and a name by which it may be referenced within the method. For example, parameters for text and a number, like this:

static void setUser(string name , int age) { *statements* **}**

When a method with parameters is called, the caller must normally pass the correct number of argument values of the required data type. These are listed within the parentheses of the calling statement – for example, calling the method defined above:

setUser("Alison" , 18) ;

Optionally, the parameter declaration may be assigned a default value to use if no argument value is passed by the caller. In this case, the caller may pass or omit an argument value:

static void setUser(string name , int age = 21) { statements }

setUser("Brenda" , 19) ;
setUser("Christine") ;   // Age will be 21.

There are three ways to pass arguments into methods:

- **By Value** – Arguments passed to methods "by value" assign a copy of the original value to the parameter. Changes made to the parameter inside the method <u>do not</u> affect the original value.

- **By Reference** – Arguments passed to methods "by reference" assign the address of the memory location of the original value to the parameter. Changes made to the parameter inside the method <u>do</u> affect the original value. Reference arguments must include the C# **ref** keyword in both the method call parentheses and the method definition parameter list.

- **For Output** – Arguments passed to methods "for output" assign the address of the memory location of the argument to the parameter, to which the method can assign a value. This is similar to passing an argument by reference except that data is passed from the method, rather than to the method. Output arguments must include the C# **out** keyword in both the method call parentheses and the method definition parameter list. This is useful to return more than one value from a method.

Beware

Calling a method without passing required arguments, or arguments of the wrong data type, will cause an error.

Hot tip

Most method calls pass arguments by value rather than by reference or for output.

1 Start a new **Console Application**, then name the project and Console.**Title** as "Parameter"

Parameter

2 Type these statements to declare two variables
```
double weight ;
string num ;
```

3 After the **Main( )** method, add this method definition to output a double value and to return a string value
```
static string getWeight( out double theWeight )
{
  theWeight = 10 ;
  return "Ten" ;
}
```

4 Next, add a method definition that returns a multiplied value of its parameter argument
```
static double lbToKg( double pounds = 5 )
{ return ( pounds * 0.45359237 ) ; }
```

Don't forget

The default parameter value is not used here as the caller passes in an argument value.

63

5 Now, add a method definition that assigns a divided value to its parameter reference argument
```
static void kgToLb( ref double weight )
{ weight = ( weight / 0.45359237 ) ; }
```

6 Finally, add statements within the **Main( )** method to pass arguments to each of the methods declared above
```
num = getWeight( out weight ) ;
Console.WriteLine( num +" lb = " + lbToKg(weight) +" kg" ) ;
kgToLb( ref weight ) ;
Console.WriteLine( num + " kg = " + weight + " lb" ) ;
Console.ReadKey( ) ;
```

Hot tip

Both the **num** and **weight** variables are initialized by the **getWeight( )** method. A reference to the **weight** variable is passed later to assign it a new value.

7 Press **Start** or **F5** to run the application and see the output featuring arguments passed to method parameters

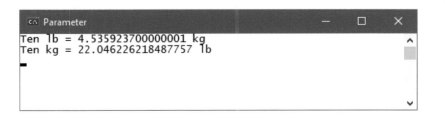

```
Parameter                                      —    □    ×
Ten lb = 4.535923700000001 kg
Ten kg = 22.046226218487757 lb
```

Overloading methods

Method "overloading" allows methods of the same name to happily co-exist in the same program, providing their parameters differ in number, data type, or both number and data type. The compiler matches a method call to the correct version of the method by recognizing its parameter number and data types – a process known as "method resolution". There are some points to consider when creating overloaded methods:

- Where a parameter represents the same value as that in another method, the parameters should have the same name.

- Parameters with the same name should appear in the same position in each method's parameter list.

- You should not use **ref** or **out** modifiers to overload methods.

It is useful to create overloaded methods when the tasks they are to perform are similar, yet subtly different.

Overload

Beware

Method definitions that only differ by their return data type cannot be overloaded – it's the parameters that must differ. Method resolution does not take return data types into consideration.

1 Start a new **Console Application**, then name the project and Console.**Title** as "Overload"

2 After the **Main()** method, add this method definition to return the calculated area of a circle
```
static double computeArea( double width )
{
  double radius = width / 2 ;
  return ( ( radius * radius ) * 3.141593 ) ;
}
```

3 Next, add a method definition to return the calculated area of a square
```
static double computeArea( double width, double height )
{
  return ( width * height ) ;
}
```

4 Then, add a method definition to return the calculated area of a triangle
```
static double
computeArea( double width, double height , char letter )
{
  return ( ( width / 2 ) * height ) ;
}
```

5 Now, turn your attention to the **Main( )** method and begin by declaring two floating-point variables
double num ;
double area ;

6 Next, add statements to initialize the first variable from user input
Console.Write("Please Enter Dimension In Feet: ") ;
num = Convert.ToDouble(Console.ReadLine( )) ;

Remember that the **ReadLine( )** method returns a **string** value – so this must be converted in order to perform arithmetic.

7 Now, initialize the second variable by calling the method that accepts only one argument and displays its value
area = computeArea(num) ;
Console.WriteLine("\nCircle:\t\tArea = "+area+" sq.ft.") ;

8 Assign a new value to the second variable by calling the method that accepts two arguments and displays its value
area = computeArea(num , num) ;
Console.WriteLine("Square:\t\tArea = "+area+" sq.ft.") ;

9 Assign another value to the second variable by calling the method that accepts three arguments and displays its value
area = computeArea(num , num , 'T') ;
Console.WriteLine("Triangle:\tArea = "+area+" sq.ft.") ;
Console.ReadKey( ) ;

The value passed to the **char letter** parameter is never used here – it is included merely to determine which method should be called.

10 Press **Start** or **F5** to run the application, then enter a number and see the output from the overloaded methods

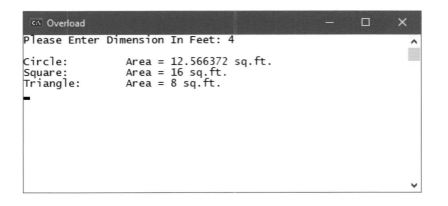

```
C:\ Overload                                    —    □    ×
Please Enter Dimension In Feet: 4

Circle:         Area = 12.566372 sq.ft.
Square:         Area = 16 sq.ft.
Triangle:       Area = 8 sq.ft.
```

Refactoring code

Methods can call themselves recursively, to repeatedly execute the statements contained in their method body – much like a loop. As with loops, a recursive method must contain an updater and a conditional test to call itself again, or stop repeating when a condition is met. The syntax of a recursive method looks like this:

```
return-data-type method-name ( parameter-list )
{
        statements-to-be-executed ;
        updater ;
        conditional-test-to-recall-or-exit ;
}
```

The updater will change the value of a passed argument – so subsequent calls will pass the adjusted value back to the method:

Refactor

1 Start a new **Console Application**, then name the project and Console.**Title** as "Refactor"

2 After the **Main()** method, add this recursive method to return the factorial value of an integer argument
```
static int factorial( int num )
{
  int result ;
  if( num == 1 )
  {
    result = 1 ;
  }
  else
  {
    result = ( factorial( num - 1 ) * num ) ;
  }
  return result ;
}
```

Hot tip

The two calls to write output in Step 3 could be refactored into a single **WriteLine( )** call for greater efficiency.

3 Next, add a method to display a range of integers and their computed factorial values
```
static void computeFactorials( int num, int max )
{
  while( num <= max )
  {
    Console.Write( "Factorial Of " + num + " : " ) ;
    Console.WriteLine( factorial( num ) ) ;
    num++ ;
  }
}
```

4 Now, add statements within the **Main( )** method to pass a
range of argument values to be computed for display
computeFactorials(1 , 8) ;
Console.**ReadKey( ) ;**

5 Press **Start** or **F5** to run the application to see the output

```
c:\ Refactor                          —   □   ×
Factorial Of 1 :1
Factorial Of 2 :2
Factorial Of 3 :6
Factorial Of 4 :24
Factorial Of 5 :120
Factorial Of 6 :720
Factorial Of 7 :5040
Factorial Of 8 :40320
■
```

If you accidentally run an
infinite recursive function,
press the **Ctrl** + **C** keys
to terminate the process.

The output lists factorial values (factorial 3 is 3x2x1=6, etc.)
but the program can be optimized by refactoring the recursive
factorial( ) method. This method does not need a variable if
written with the ternary operator:

6 Edit the **factorial( )** method listed in Step 2 to make it
more efficient
```
static int factorial( int num )
{
  return ( num == 1 ) ? 1 : ( factorial( num - 1 ) * num ) ;
}
```

A recursive method
generally uses more
system resources than a
loop – but it can make
the code more readable.

7 Press **Start** or **F5** to run the application once more and
see the same output, produced more efficiently

```
c:\ Refactor                          —   □   ×
Factorial Of 1 :1
Factorial Of 2 :2
Factorial Of 3 :6
Factorial Of 4 :24
Factorial Of 5 :120
Factorial Of 6 :720
Factorial Of 7 :5040
Factorial Of 8 :40320
■
```

Summary

- A programmer-specified method is a modular section of code that can be called to execute its statements whenever required.

- It is easier to understand, maintain, re-use, and share modular program code that contains methods.

- A method declaration must at least specify a return data type and the method name.

- Methods not intended for use by other classes must be initialized in memory by the **static** keyword.

- Optionally, a method declaration may include a parameter list.

- Variables declared within a method have local scope by default, so are not accessible from outside that method.

- Arguments passed by value assign a copy of the original value to the method parameter, so the original will not be affected.

- Arguments passed by reference assign a memory location to the method parameter, so the original value will be affected.

- Arguments passed for output retrieve a value from the method and are useful to return more than one value.

- Method overloading allows methods of the same name to co-exist in the same program if their parameters differ.

- The compiler matches calls to overloaded methods by recognizing their parameter number and data types.

- Parameters representing the same values in overloaded methods should have the same name and the same position.

- The reference **ref** and output **out** modifiers should not be used with overloaded methods.

- Code can be refactored for optimum efficiency by reducing the number of variables and method calls.

- Recursive methods repeatedly execute their statements, so must contain an updater to stop repeating at some point.

6 Handling strings

This chapter demonstrates how to manipulate and format text strings within C# programs.

Discovering string features

The C# **String** class library provides properties and methods that enable a program to easily discover features of a text string. Usefully, the **String.IsNullOrWhiteSpace( )** and **String.IsNullOrEmpty( )** methods can be used to validate user input. These are **static** methods, so are written dot-suffixed to the **String** class name.

Other properties and methods operate on an "instance" of the class, so are written dot-suffixed to a **string** variable name. Instance methods can report **string** size and query its contents. The **Length** property returns an integer that is the number of characters within the string, including spaces. Additionally, the **StartsWith( )**, **EndsWith( )**, and **Contains( )** methods can each accept a string argument to match within the **string** variable value. When a match is found, they return **true**, otherwise they return **false**:

Hot tip

String class methods can be written using the **String.** class prefix or its **string.** alias prefix – our examples use **String** to differentiate from the **string** data type.

Features

Hot tip

Methods with a **String.** (or **string.**) prefix are using the **String** class itself, whereas dot-suffixed methods use an "instance" object of the class – see Chapter 9.

Beware

Note that some of these strings include ' single quotes within the outer " double quote marks.

1   Start a new **Console Application**, then name the project and **Console.Title** as "Features"

2   Type these statements requesting user input to initialize a string variable
```
Console.Write( "Please Enter Text: " ) ;
string text = Console.ReadLine( ) ;
```

3   Next, add a conditional test to ensure the user entered input before hitting the **Enter** key
```
if ( String.IsNullOrWhiteSpace( text ) )
{
  Console.WriteLine( "\nERROR: No Text Found!" ) ;
}
else
{
  // Statements to be inserted here (Steps 4-7).
}
Console.ReadKey( ) ;
```

4   Now, insert statements to report the length of the string
```
Console.WriteLine( "\nThanks. You Entered:\n'"+text+"'" ) ;
Console.WriteLine( "\nText Length: " + text.Length ) ;
```

5   Insert another statement to test how the string begins
```
string query = text.StartsWith( "C#" ) ? "Does" : "Does Not" ;
Console.WriteLine( "Text " + query + " Start With 'C#'" ) ;
```

6 Next, insert a statement to test how the string ends
```
query = text.EndsWith( "steps" ) ? "Does" : "Does Not" ;
Console.WriteLine( "Text " + query + " End With 'steps'" ) ;
```

7 Now, insert a statement to test what the string contains
```
query = text.Contains( "easy" ) ? "Does" : "Does Not" ;
Console.WriteLine( "Text " + query + " Contain 'easy'" ) ;
```

8 Press **Start** or **F5** to run the application, and hit **Enter** without input to see the error message

```
CN Features                                    —    □    ×
Please Enter Text:

ERROR: No Text Found!
```

9 Press **Start** or **F5** to run the application again, type input, then hit **Enter** to discover input string features

```
CN Features                                    —    □    ×
Please Enter Text: C# Programming in easy steps

Thanks. You Entered:
'C# Programming in easy steps'

Text Length: 28
Text Does Start With 'C#'
Text Does End With 'steps'
Text Does Contain 'easy'
```

```
CN Features                                    —    □    ×
Please Enter Text: Java in easy steps

Thanks. You Entered:
'Java in easy steps'

Text Length: 18
Text Does Not Start With 'C#'
Text Does End With 'steps'
Text Does Contain 'easy'
```

Notice that the **?:** ternary operator is used here to assign an appropriate **string** value.

String values are often referred to as "literals", as they comprise characters to be read literally, as text.

Manipulating strings

The C# String class library provides methods that enable a program to manipulate text strings. The **ToLower( )** and **ToUpper( )** methods can be dot-suffixed to a **string** variable to change all characters within the string to lowercase, or to uppercase.

Similarly, the **TrimStart( )**, **TrimEnd( )**, and **Trim( )** methods can be used to remove whitespace or other characters from a **string** at its start, end, or both start and end. By default, these methods will remove whitespace from the string, but you can alternatively specify a character to be removed as an argument to the method.

Conversely, the **PadLeft( )** and **PadRight( )** methods can be used to add whitespace or other characters onto a **string** at its start or end. Their arguments must specify the total character length of the padded string, and a padding character unless default whitespace padding is required. If you want to add padding onto both start and end, the methods can be "chained" as **PadLeft( ).PadRight( )** stating each padding length argument, and character if required:

Hot tip

You can also specify multiple characters to be trimmed as a comma-separated list of arguments to the **TrimStart()**, **TrimEnd()**, or **Trim()** methods.

Manipulate

1 Start a new **Console Application**, then name the project and Console.**Title** as "Manipulate"

2 Type these statements requesting user input to initialize a string variable
```
Console.Write( "Please Enter Text: " ) ;
string text = Console.ReadLine( ) ;
```

3 Add statements to display the user input string and report its length
```
Console.Write( "\nThanks. You Entered:\n'" + text + "'" ) ;
Console.WriteLine( "\t\tText Length: " + text.Length ) ;
```

Hot tip

It is a good idea to always use **Trim( )** to remove spaces accidentally added by the user when typing input.

4 Remove leading and trailing whitespace, then display the manipulated version and report its length
```
text = text.Trim( ) ;
Console.Write( "\nTrimmed:\t'" + text + "'" ) ;
Console.WriteLine( "\tText Length: " + text.Length ) ;
```

5 Next, add statements to create and display an uppercase version of the trimmed string
```
string upper = text.ToUpper( ) ;
Console.WriteLine( "\nUpperCase:\t'" + upper + "'" ) ;
```

6 Now, create and display a lowercase version of the trimmed string
```
string lower = text.ToLower( ) ;
Console.WriteLine( "LowerCase:\t'" + lower + "'" ) ;
```

7 Then, further manipulate all three strings to add whitespace and character padding
```
upper = upper.PadLeft( 40 ) ;
lower = lower.PadRight( 40 , '#' ) ;
text = text.PadLeft( 30 , '*' ).PadRight( 40 , '*' ) ;
```

Here, all three strings are expanded to a total width of 40 characters.

8 Add statements to display all three strings to see the padded whitespace and padded characters
```
Console.WriteLine( "\nPadded Left:\t'" + upper + "'" ) ;
Console.WriteLine( "Padded Right:\t'" + lower + "'" ) ;
Console.WriteLine( "Padded Both:\t'" + text + "'" ) ;
```

9 Finally, add statements to display trimmed versions of two padded strings
```
Console.WriteLine( "\nTrimmed Start:\t'" +
                        upper.TrimStart( ) + "'" ) ;
Console.WriteLine( "Trimmed End:\t'" +
                        text.TrimEnd( '*' ) + "'" ) ;
Console.ReadKey( ) ;
```

10 Press **Start** or **F5** to run the application and enter a string with leading and trailing space to see it manipulated

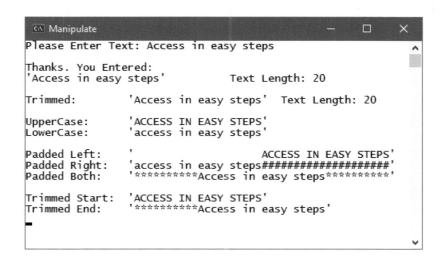

When padding both left and right you must individually specify by how much to expand the string in each direction – in this case, expanding from 20 to 30 characters left, then from 30 to 40 characters right.

Joining and comparing strings

When the **+** operator is used to concatenate (join) strings in an assignment, the combined strings get stored in the **string** variable. But when used in the **Write( )** or **WriteLine( )** methods, the strings are only combined in output – the variable values are unchanged.

The C# String class library provides a String.**Concat( )** method that can be used to join strings as an alternative to using the **+** operator. This method accepts a comma-separated list of **string** arguments to be joined into a single **string**.

Similarly, the String.**Join( )** method can also be used to join strings as an alternative to using the **+** operator. This, too, accepts a comma-separated list of **string** arguments to be joined, but its first argument usefully specifies a separator **string**. It places this separator between each other **string** argument in the joined **string**. The separator might be a single space to separate words, or perhaps an HTML tag to separate text, or any other **string** value.

String comparisons can be made for alphabetic order by specifying two string arguments to the String.**Compare( )** method. This returns an integer denoting whether the alphabetic relationship of the first string to the second is before (**-1**), after (**1**), or equal (**0**). There is also a **CompareTo( )** method that provides the same results, but this can be dot-suffixed onto the first string, and the second string specified as its argument.

As with numeric comparisons, the **==** operator can be used to test for string equality. Alternatively, the **Equals( )** method can be dot-suffixed onto the first string, and the second string specified as its argument. Either will return a **true** or **false** Boolean result.

Hot tip

The examples in this book use the **+** operator for concatenation rather than String.**Concat( )** as it provides better readability without any loss of performance.

Joined

1 Start a new **Console Application**, then name the project and Console.**Title** as "Joined"

2 Type this statement to create and initialize a **string** array variable simply named "a"
```
string [ ] a = new string[ 3 ] { "Alpha", "Bravo", "Charlie" } ;
```

3 Next, assign a concatenated version of the first two array element values to a **string** variable and display its value
```
string s = String.Concat( a[0] , a[1] ) ;
Console.WriteLine( "Concatenated:\t" + s ) ;
```

4 Assign a joined version of the first two array elements and space separator to the string variable, then display its value
```
s = String.Join( " " , a[0] , a[1] ) ;
Console.WriteLine( "Joined:\t\t" + s ) ;
```

5 Assign a joined version of all three array elements and tag separator to the string variable, then display its value
```
s = String.Join( "<br>" , a ) ;
Console.WriteLine( "\nHTML:\t" + s +"\n" ) ;
```

Notice how only the array name needs to be specified as the argument to join all three array elements.

6 Next, add statements to compare, in turn, all three array elements for alphabetic order
```
int num = String.Compare( a[0] , a[1] ) ;
Console.WriteLine( a[0] + " v " + a[1] + ":\t" + num ) ;

num = String.Compare( a[2] , a[1] ) ;
Console.WriteLine( a[2] + " v " + a[1] + ":\t" + num ) ;

num = a[1].CompareTo( a[1] ) ;
Console.WriteLine( a[1]+ " v "+a[1]+":\t" + num+"\n" ) ;
```

You can add or remove the \t escape sequences to format the output to your liking.

7 Finally, test the array element values for equality
```
bool flag = ( a[0] == a[1] ) ;
Console.WriteLine( a[0]+" == "+a[1]+":\t\t" + flag ) ;
flag = a[2].Equals( a[2] ) ;
Console.WriteLine( a[2]+" == "+a[2]+":\t\t" + flag ) ;
Console.ReadKey( ) ;
```

8 Press **Start** or **F5** to run the application to see the joined strings and comparison results

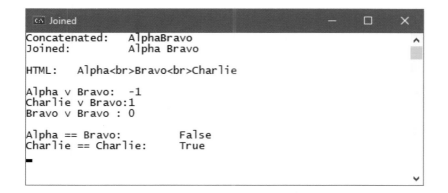

Two alternative methods are used here to compare strings and to test for equality.

Copying and swapping strings

The C# **String** class library provides a **String.Copy( )** method that can be used to copy one string to another string as an alternative to using the = assignment operator. This method accepts the **string** to be copied as its argument. Perhaps more usefully, the **CopyTo( )** method can be dot-suffixed onto a **string** variable to copy its contents into a **char** character array. This requires four arguments to specify the index number from which to start copying in the source **string**, the name of the **char** array, the index number at which to start copying in the destination **char** array, and the number of characters to copy.

Other methods can be dot-suffixed to a **string** variable to swap its contents. The **Remove( )** method requires an integer argument to specify the index number at which to begin removing characters from the **string**. This will remove all characters from the specified index position up to the end of the **string**, unless you add a second argument to specify the number of characters to be removed.

Conversely, the **Insert( )** method requires an integer argument to specify the index number at which to begin inserting characters into the **string**, and an argument specifying the **string** to insert. The **Replace( )** method simply requires two **string** arguments to specify a substring to seek within the **string**, and a **string** to replace that substring when a match is found:

Hot tip

Copying with an = assignment produces two **string** variables that contain the same value and reference the <u>same</u> memory location, whereas copying with the **String.Copy( )** method produces two **string** variables that contain the same value but reference <u>different</u> memory locations.

76

C#

Copied

1 Start a new **Console Application**, then name the project and **Console.Title** as "Copied"

2 Type these statements to create and initialize two **string** variables with the names of two Maserati car models
```
string car1 = "Ghibli" ;
string car2 = "GranTurismo" ;
```

3 Next, display the original values contained in each variable
```
Console.WriteLine( "Original:" ) ;
Console.WriteLine( "\tCar 1: "+ car1 +" \t\tCar 2: " + car2 ) ;
```

4 Now, copy the value of the second **string** variable into the first **string** variable and display their modified values
```
car1 = String.Copy( car2 ) ;
Console.WriteLine( "\nCopied:" ) ;
Console.WriteLine( "\tCar 1: "+ car1 + "\tCar 2: " + car2 ) ;
```

5 Initialize an integer variable with the length of the first **string** variable, then create a character array of that length
```
int num = car1.Length ;
char [ ] model = new char [ num ] ;
```

6 Next, copy the first **string** variable into the character array, then display a space-separated list of the element contents
```
car1.CopyTo( 0 , model , 0 , num ) ;
Console.WriteLine( "\nCharacter Array:" ) ;
foreach( char c in model ) { Console.Write( c + " " ) ; }
```

7 Now, remove the end of the first **string** variable, starting from its fifth element, and display the modified value
```
car1 = car1.Remove( 4 ) ;
Console.WriteLine( "\n\nRemoved... \tCar 1: " + car1 ) ;
```

8 Insert two strings into the first **string** variable, at its beginning and end, then display the modified value
```
car1 = car1.Insert( 0 , "Maserati " ) ;
car1 = car1.Insert( 13 , "Cabrio" ) ;
Console.WriteLine( "\nInserted... \tCar 1: " + car1 ) ;
```

9 Finally, replace a substring within the first **string** variable, and once more display the modified value
```
car1 = car1.Replace( "GranCabrio" , "Quattroporte" ) ;
Console.WriteLine( "\nReplaced... \tCar 1: " + car1 ) ;
Console.ReadKey( ) ;
```

10 Press **Start** or **F5** to run the application to see the copied and swapped strings

The **char** array must be of the same size as the **string** to be copied – use the string's **Length** property to specify the size of the **char** array.

The fifth element of an array is at index position 4 in a zero-based index.

```
C:\ Copied                                              —    □   ×
Original:        Car 1: Ghibli          Car 2: GranTurismo  ▲
Copied:          Car 1: GranTurismo     Car 2: GranTurismo
Character Array: G r a n T u r i s m o
Removed...       Car 1: Gran
Inserted...      Car 1: Maserati GranCabrio
Replaced...      Car 1: Maserati Quattroporte
▬
                                                           ▼
```

The position reported when a substring is found is the index position of the first character of that substring within the searched string – whether searching forwards or backwards.

78

Substring

Finding substrings

The C# String class library provides a number of methods that can be dot-suffixed to a **string** variable to seek a string within a **string** (i.e. a "substring"). The **IndexOf( )** method requires the substring as its argument and, if found, returns the index position of the substring within the searched **string**. Otherwise, it will return **-1**. The **IndexOf( )** method searches forwards, from left-to-right, and returns the index position of the first occurrence of the substring. It has a companion **LastIndexOf( )** method that works in just the same way, but searches backwards, from right-to-left.

Similarly, there is an **IndexOfAny( )** method and its companion **LastIndexOfAny( )** method that require a character array argument. These seek any character of the specified array within a string, and return the index position of the first occurrence, or **-1** otherwise.

You can also dot-suffix a **Substring( )** method to a **string** variable if you want to extract a copy of a substring from within that **string**. This method requires two arguments to specify the index position at which to begin copying, and the number of characters to copy:

1 Start a new **Console Application**, then name the project and Console.**Title** as "Substring"

2 After the **Main( )** method, add this method declaration to report the result of a substring search
```
static void report( int pos , string sub )
{
  if( pos != -1 )
  { Console.WriteLine( "'" + sub + "' Found At " + pos ) ; }
  else
  { Console.WriteLine( "'" + sub + "' Not Found!" ) ; }
}
```

3 Now, turn your attention to the **Main( )** method and initialize a **string** variable, then display its value and length
```
string text = "My dog is a cute dog" ;
Console.WriteLine( text + "\tLength: " + text.Length ) ;
```

4 Next, request user input to initialize another string variable with a substring to seek
```
Console.WriteLine( "\nPlease Enter A Substring To Seek: " ) ;
string sub = Console.ReadLine( ) ;
```

5 Create a character array and copy the entire substring value into the character array
```
char [ ] arr = new char[ sub.Length ] ;
sub.CopyTo( 0 , arr , 0 , sub.Length ) ;
```

The **CopyTo( )** method is described and demonstrated in the previous example on pages 76-77.

6 Then, seek the first occurrence of the substring and call the method you defined to report the search result
```
int pos = text.IndexOf( sub ) ;
report( pos , sub ) ;
```

7 Now, seek the last occurrence of the substring and report the result
```
pos = text.LastIndexOf( sub ) ;
report( pos , sub ) ;
```

8 Next, seek the first occurrence of any character of the substring and report the result
```
pos = text.IndexOfAny( arr ) ;
report( pos , text.Substring( pos , 1 ) ) ;
```

Notice that a copy of the located character is extracted from the original **string** using the **Substring( )** method for output in the report.

9 Finally, seek the last occurrence of any character of the substring and report the result
```
pos = text.LastIndexOfAny( arr ) ;
report( pos , text.Substring( pos , 1 ) ) ;
Console.ReadKey( ) ;
```

10 Press **Start** or **F5** to run the application, then enter a substring to seek and see the reported results

79

Formatting strings

In C# every object has a **ToString( )** method that returns a string representation of that object. This means that the **ToString( )** method can be dot-suffixed to any numeric variable to get its value represented in **string** format. The **ToString( )** method can, optionally, accept a string argument to specify how the **string** version should be formatted. Common specifiers are listed below:

Specifier	Returns
G	General
F	Fixed Point
N	Number (with comma-separated thousands)
C	Currency (prevailing on your system)
P	Percentage (multiplied by 100)
00.0000	Zero Padding

The C# **String** class library provides a **String.Format( )** method that uses the same specifiers to also produce values represented in **string** format. This requires an argument to specify the **string** to be formatted, which may include "placeholders", and an argument list to be substituted for each placeholder in the output **string**.

Each placeholder can be numbered sequentially (starting at zero) within **{ }** braces, to match the list position of the substitution argument. For example, **{0}** matches the first argument in the substitution argument list, **{1}** matches the second, and so on. Additionally, the number may be followed by a **:** colon and one of the format specifiers in the table above – to specify how the substituted value should appear in its **string** – for example, **{0:G}**.

Data strings that contain separators, such as a comma-separated list of data retrieved from a database query, can be easily broken into individual items of data by dot-suffixing the **Split( )** method to a **string** variable. The individual strings can be assigned to a **string** array variable, and could then be formatted in output by the **String.Format( )** method if required.

The C# specifications provide further string formatting specifier options in addition to the commonly used ones shown here.

Multiple placeholders in one string can be numbered alike – if you want each one to be substituted by the same list argument value.

...cont'd

1 Start a new **Console Application**, then name the project and Console.**Title** as "Format"

Format

2 Initialize a numeric variable, then use the **ToString()** method to output its value as a currency **string** format

```
double sum = 2500 ;
Console.WriteLine( "Currency String: " + sum.ToString( "C" ) ) ;
```

3 Next, use the String.**Format()** method to output the same numeric value in various common **string** formats

```
Console.Write( String.Format( "\nGeneral:\t {0:G}" , sum ) ) ;
Console.Write( String.Format( "\nFixed Point:\t {0:F}", sum ) ) ;
Console.Write( String.Format( "\nNumber:\t\t {0:N}" , sum ) ) ;
Console.Write( String.Format( "\nCurrency:\t {0:C}" , sum ) ) ;
```

The specifier letters may be written as either uppercase or lowercase.

4 Now, reduce the numeric value, then output it in a percentage **string** format and with padded zeros

```
sum /= 1000 ;
Console.Write( String.Format( "\nPercentage:\t {0:P}", sum ) ) ;
Console.Write
( String.Format( "\nZero Padded:\t {0:00.0000} \n", sum ) ) ;
```

81

5 Then, create a comma-separated **string** list and split it into individual elements of a **string** array variable for output

```
string data = "Mike,McGrath,Author" ;

string [ ] items = data.Split( ',' ) ;
foreach ( string item in items )
{ Console.Write( String.Format( "\n* {0}" , item ) ) ; }
Console.ReadKey( ) ;
```

Beware

The argument to the **Split( )** method must be a single **char** character – enclosed in <u>single</u> quotes.

6 Press **Start** or **F5** to see the formatted string output

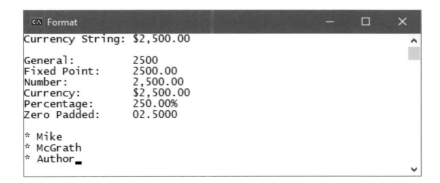

```
C:\ Format                                    —  □  ×
Currency String: $2,500.00
                                                      ^
General:         2500
Fixed Point:     2500.00
Number:          2,500.00
Currency:        $2,500.00
Percentage:      250.00%
Zero Padded:     02.5000

* Mike
* McGrath
* Author_
                                                      v
```

Don't forget

You can use the + concatenation operator for formatting, but many prefer String.**Format( )** for easily readable code.

You can use IntelliSense to choose methods and properties – for example, type DateTime.**Now.** and select from the pop-up list that appears.

The C# specifications provide further date and time formatting specifier options in addition to the commonly used ones shown here.

Formatting date strings

The C# DateTime class library provides methods and properties to easily work with dates and times. Its **Now** property returns a DateTime object of the current local date and time of your system. Alternatively, you can create a DateTime object using the **new** keyword, and specifying a date and time as a comma-separated list of arguments. Many methods and properties can be dot-suffixed to any DateTime object to specify its format, or to extract specific components of the date or time, or to modify its value. For example, the **DayOfWeek** property supplies the day name, the **ToShortString( )** method supplies the date in number form, and the **AddYears( )** method can modify the year component.

The String.**Format( )** method, introduced in the previous example on pages 80-81, also has these specifiers that can be used to determine the format of dates and times in output:

Specifier	Returns	Example
d	Short date	7/4/2023
D	Long date	**Tuesday, July 4, 2023**
t	Short time	**8:15 AM**
T	Long time	**8:15:30 AM**
f	Full datetime	**Tuesday, July 4, 2023 8:15 AM**
F	Full+seconds	**Tuesday, July 4, 2023 8:15:30 AM**
M	Month+day	**July 4**
Y	Month+year	**July 2023**
dd	Day number	**04**
dddd	Day name	**Tuesday**
HH	Hour 0-23	**08**
mm	Minute	**15**
ss	Second	**30**
YYYY	Year	**2023**

1 Start a new **Console Application,** then name the project and Console.**Title** as "DateFormat"

DateFormat

2 Initialize a DateTime object and display its value
DateTime **now** = DateTime.**Now** ;
Console.**Write**("Current Date And Time: "+ **now**) ;

3 Next, display specific components of the DateTime object
Console.**Write**("\nDay Name: "+ **now.DayOfWeek**) ;
Console.**Write**("\nDate Only: "+ **now.ToShortDateString( )**) ;
Console.**Write**("\nTime Only: "+ **now.ToShortTimeString( )**) ;

4 Modify the DateTime object and display its new value
now = **now.AddYears(4)** ;
Console.**Write**("\n\nFuture Date: "+ **now**) ;

5 Now, create a new DateTime object and display its value
DateTime **dt** = **new** DateTime**(2025, 7, 4, 8, 15, 30)** ;
Console.**Write**("\n\nSet Date And Time: {0:f}", **dt**) ;

6 Display specific components of the new DateTime object
Console.**Write**("\nDay Name: {0:dddd}", **dt**) ;
Console.**Write**("\nLong Date: {0:D}", **dt**) ;
Console.**Write**("\nLong Time: {0:T}", **dt**) ;
Console.**ReadKey( )** ;

7 Press **Start** or **F5** to run the application and see the formatted date and time output

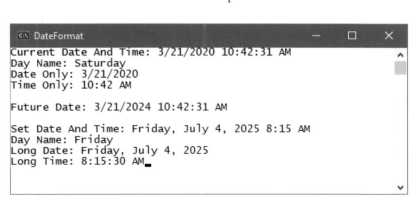

Hot tip

You need only specify the date components when creating a new DateTime object – the time will automatically be set to 12:00 AM (midnight).

Summary

- Class library **static** methods, such as String.**IsNullOrEmpty( )**, are dot-suffixed onto the String class library name.

- String values can be joined using the String.**Concat( )** and String.**Join( )** methods, or by using the **+** concatenation operator.

- String comparisons can be made for alphabetic order using the String.**Compare( )** method.

- A value can be copied from one **string** variable to another using the String.**Copy( )** method, or the **=** assignment operator.

- The String.**Format( )** method can be used to format both numeric and date strings in output.

- The DateTime class library provides methods and properties, such as **Now**, to work with date and time strings.

- Instance methods and properties, such as **Contains( )** and **Length**, are dot-suffixed onto **string** variable names.

- The character case of a **string** value can be changed using the **ToLower( )** and **ToUpper( )** methods.

- Whitespace or other characters can be removed from a **string** value using the **TrimStart( )**, **TrimEnd( )**, and **Trim( )** methods.

- Whitespace or other characters can be added to a **string** value using the **PadLeft( )** and **PadRight( )** methods.

- String comparisons can be made using the **CompareTo( )** and **Equals( )** methods, or the **==** equality operator.

- A **string** value can be copied from a **string** variable into a **char** array using the **CopyTo( )** method.

- The contents of a string variable can be swapped using the **Remove( )**, **Insert( )**, and **Replace( )** methods.

- A substring can be sought using **IndexOf( )**, **LastIndexOf( )**, **IndexOfAny( )**, **LastIndexOfAny( )**, and **Substring( )** methods.

- Every object has a **ToString( )** method that returns a string representation, which can be formatted in output.

7 Accessing files

This chapter demonstrates how C# programs can store data in text files, and retrieve data from text files.

Writing a file

The C# **System.IO**.File class library provides methods that enable a program to easily write text into a file on your computer. The **System.IO** class is not automatically listed in the default **using** directive generated by Visual Studio. This means you must include the **System.IO** prefix when using File methods or, more conveniently, add a further **using** directive so the prefix may then be omitted in your program code:

using System.IO ;

The File.**WriteAllText( )** method simply requires two arguments to specify the text file path and the string to write. Backslash characters in the path string must be escaped to avoid an error.

If you would like to ensure the specified text file does not already exist, you can first test for its existence by specifying its path as the argument to the File.**Exists( )** method. This will return **true** when the file is found, otherwise it will return **false**.

In order to ensure the text file was written successfully, it is worthwhile wrapping the File.**WriteAllText( )** call in a **try-catch** block. A statement confirming success can be included in the **try** part of the block, and a statement to advise of failure can be included in the **catch** part of the block:

Beware

If you don't add the **using System.IO ;** statement you must write **System.IO.File. WriteAllText( )** and **System.IO.File.Exists( )** to call these methods.

WriteText

1 Start a new **Console Application**, then name the project and Console.**Title** as "WriteText"

2 Type this directive above the **namespace** declaration to make a further class library available to the program **using System.IO ;**

3 Back in the **Main( )** method, add these statements to initialize two variables – insert your own user name where indicated in the path

```
// Edit the line below to include your user name.
string path = "C:\\Users\\username\\Desktop\\poem.txt" ;
string poem = "\r\n\tI never saw a man who looked" ;
poem += "\r\n\tWith such a wistful eye" ;
poem += "\r\n\tUpon that little tent of blue" ;
poem += "\r\n\tWhich prisoners call the sky" ;
```

Don't forget

The \r\n\t escape sequence is a carriage return, a newline, and a tab.

4 Next, add a statement to test if a file already exists of the specified path and filename

```
if( File.Exists( path )  )
{
  Console.WriteLine( "File Already Exists: " + path ) ;
}
else
{
  // Statements to be inserted here (Step 5).
}
Console.ReadKey( ) ;
```

5 Now, insert statements that attempt to write a text file and confirm success, or advise of failure

```
try
{
  File.WriteAllText( path , poem ) ;
  Console.WriteLine( "File Written: " + path ) ;
}
catch( Exception error )
{
  Console.WriteLine( error.Message ) ;
}
```

Hot tip

Catching exceptions with the **try-catch** block is fully described in Chapter 8, dealing with problem solving – see pages 106-107.

6 Press **Start** or **F5** to run the application and see a text file written on your Desktop, or see an error message

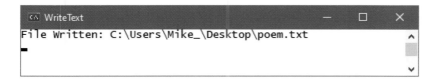

Hot tip

Run this application again to see the message advising that the file already exists.

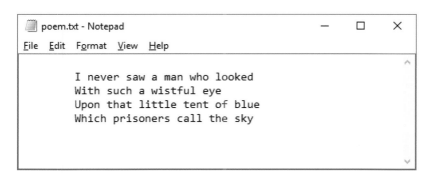

Appending to a file

The C# **System.IO**.File class library provides a **WriteAllLines( )** method that can be used to write the contents of a **string** array to a text file, with each element appearing on a separate line, and a **try-catch** block can ensure the text file was written successfully.

Additionally, the **System.IO**.File class has an **AppendAllText( )** method, which can be used to add text to an existing file, and the File.**Exists( )** method can ensure that the file first exists:

AppendText

Don't forget

The \r\n character return, newline escape sequences can be omitted from the **string** array, as the **WriteAllLines( )** method automatically writes each element on new lines.

1 Start a new **Console Application**, then name the project and Console.**Title** as "AppendText"

2 Type this directive above the **namespace** declaration to make a further class library available to the program **using System.IO** ;

3 Back in the **Main( )** method, add these statements to initialize three variables – insert your own user name where indicated in the path
```
string path = "C:\\Users\\username\\Desktop\\oscar.txt" ;
string [ ] poem = new string [ ]
{
  "\tIn Debtors' Yard the stones are hard" ,
  "\tAnd the dripping wall is high"
} ;
string attrib = "\r\n\tThe Ballad Of Reading Gaol " ;
attrib += "(Oscar Wilde 1898)" ;
```

4 Next, add a statement to test if a file already exists of the specified path and filename
```
if( File.Exists( path ) )
{
  // Statements to be inserted here (Step 5).
}
else
{
  // Statements to be inserted here (Step 6).
}
Console.ReadKey( ) ;
```

5 Now, insert statements that attempt to append text if the file already exists, and advise of success
```
  File.AppendAllText( path , attrib ) ;
  Console.WriteLine( "Appended To File: " +  path ) ;
```

6 Then, insert statements that attempt to write a text file and confirm success, or advise of failure

```
try
{
  File.WriteAllLines( path , poem ) ;
  Console.WriteLine( "File Written: " + path ) ;
}
catch( Exception error )
{
  Console.WriteLine( error.Message ) ;
}
```

As with **WriteAllText( )**, the **WriteAllLines( )** method requires the text file path and **string** to write as its arguments.

7 Press **Start** or **F5** to run the application and see a text file written on your Desktop, or see an error message

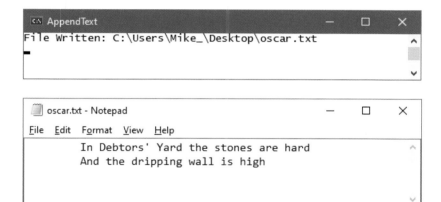

```
cs  AppendText                                    —    □    ×
File Written: C:\Users\Mike_\Desktop\oscar.txt      ^



                                                    v
```

```
oscar.txt - Notepad                               —    □    ×
File  Edit  Format  View  Help
        In Debtors' Yard the stones are hard      ^
        And the dripping wall is high


                                                  v
```

There is also an **AppendAllLines( )** method that can be used to add the contents of a **string** array to a file.

8 Run the application once more and see a confirmation appear and see text appended to the file

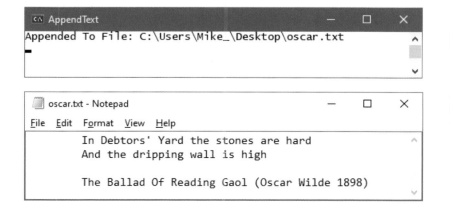

```
cs  AppendText                                    —    □    ×
Appended To File: C:\Users\Mike_\Desktop\oscar.txt  ^



                                                    v
```

```
oscar.txt - Notepad                               —    □    ×
File  Edit  Format  View  Help
        In Debtors' Yard the stones are hard      ^
        And the dripping wall is high

        The Ballad Of Reading Gaol (Oscar Wilde 1898)
                                                  v
```

After its first run, this application will append text each time it is run.

Reading text and lines

The C# **System.IO.**File class library provides a **ReadAllText( )** method that can be used to read text from an existing file and assign its entire contents to a **string** variable. The File.**Exists( )** method can ensure that the text file first exists, and a **try-catch** block can ensure the file was read successfully.

Additionally, the **System.IO.**File class has a **ReadAllLines( )** method, which can be used to assign each line of a text file to an individual element of a **string** array:

ReadText

1 Start a new **Console Application**, then name the project and Console.**Title** as "ReadText"

2 Type this directive above the **namespace** declaration to make a further class library available to the program
using System.IO ;

3 Back in the **Main( )** method, add this statement to initialize a variable – insert your own user name where indicated in the path
string path = "C:\\Users**_username_\\Desktop\\word.txt" ;**

4 Next, add a statement to test if a file already exists of the specified path and filename
```
if( File.Exists( path ) )
{
  // Statements to be inserted here (Step 5).
}
else
{
  Console.WriteLine( "File Not Found: " + path ) ;
}
Console.ReadKey( ) ;
```

When a text file is read into a **string** array, the array's **Length** property, which returns the number of its elements, will represent the number of lines read – including empty lines!

5 Now, insert a statement to display a message if the file cannot be read successfully
```
try
{
  // Statements to be inserted here (Steps 6 and 7).
}
catch( Exception error )
{
  Console.WriteLine( error.Message ) ;
}
```

6 Then, insert statements to assign the text file contents to a variable and display its value

```
string text = File.ReadAllText( path ) ;
Console.WriteLine( "File Read: " + path + "\n" ) ;
Console.WriteLine( text + "\n" ) ;
```

7 Finally, insert statements to assign the text file contents to an array variable and display each element with a counter

```
string [ ] lines = File.ReadAllLines( path ) ;
int num = 1 ;
foreach( string line in lines )
{
  Console.WriteLine( num + " : " + line ) ;
  num++ ;
}
```

The text file's invisible newline and tab characters are preserved when read by the **ReadAllText( )** method, but only the invisible tab characters are preserved when it is read by the **ReadAllLines( )** method.

8 Open a text editor such as Notepad, and create a multi-line text file named "word.txt" on your Desktop

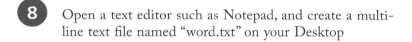

```
word.txt - Notepad                        —    □    ×

File  Edit  Format  View  Help
        Yet each man kills the thing he loves
        By each let this be heard,
        Some do it with a bitter look,
        Some with a flattering word
```

9 Press **Start** or **F5** to run the application and see a text file read from your Desktop, or see an error message

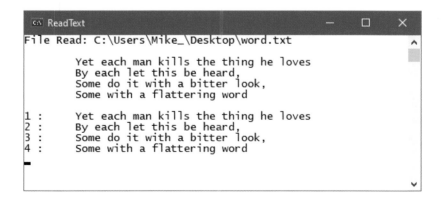

```
ReadText                                  —    □    ×

File Read: C:\Users\Mike_\Desktop\word.txt

        Yet each man kills the thing he loves
        By each let this be heard,
        Some do it with a bitter look,
        Some with a flattering word

1 :     Yet each man kills the thing he loves
2 :     By each let this be heard,
3 :     Some do it with a bitter look,
4 :     Some with a flattering word
```

Remove the text files' Read and ReadWrite permissions on your system and run the application again to see an "Access to path denied" message.

Streaming lines

The **File**.**WriteAllText( )** and **File**.**AppendAllText( )** methods are simple to use but provide few options. The **System.IO**.StreamWriter class also provides object methods that can be used to write text to a file, and these provide more options. An instance of a StreamWriter object must first be created using the **new** keyword, and the text file path specified as an argument to its "constructor" method, like this:

StreamWriter **name** = **new** StreamWriter(**path**) ;

Methods such as **Write( )** and **WriteLine( )** can then be dot-suffixed to the object name. A StreamWriter object is disposable, so its statements are best enclosed within a **using** construct to ensure it is removed from memory upon completion, like this:

using (StreamWriter **name** = **new** StreamWriter(**path**))
{
  // *Statements.*
}

The **using** construct can also be wrapped in a **try-catch** block, to ensure the text file was written successfully. Optionally, the StreamWriter constructor can accept a second argument of **true** to append to existing text:

The **using** keyword has different meanings according to its context.

WriteStream

1 Start a new **Console Application**, then name the project and Console.**Title** as "WriteStream"

2 Type this directive above the **namespace** declaration to make a further class library available to the program
using System.IO ;

3 Back in the **Main( )** method, add these statements to initialize three variables – insert your own user name where indicated in the path
string path = "C:\\Users*username*\\Desktop\\robert.txt" ;
string poem = new string [ ]
{
  "\tThis truth finds honest Tam o' Shanter" ,
  "\tAs he from Ayr one night did canter" ,
  "\tOld Ayr, which never a town surpasses" ,
  "\tFor honest men and bonny lasses."
} ;
string attrib = "\r\n\tTam o'Shanter (Robert Burns 1790)" ;

4 Next, add a statement to display a message if the file cannot be written successfully

```
try
{
  // Statements to be inserted here (Steps 5 and 6).
}
catch( Exception error )
{ Console.WriteLine( error.Message ) ; }
Console.ReadKey( ) ;
```

5 Now, insert statements that attempt to write the contents of the variable array into a text file

```
using ( StreamWriter writer = new StreamWriter( path ) )
{
  foreach( string line in poem )
  { writer.WriteLine( line ) ; }
}
```

Hot tip

The **using** construct ensures the StreamWriter is disposed of when its operations complete, so the same name can be used for the new object.

6 Finally, insert statements that attempt to append the contents of the regular variable into a text file

```
using ( StreamWriter writer =
                      new StreamWriter( path, true )  )
{
  writer.WriteLine( attrib ) ;
  Console.WriteLine( "File Written: " + path ) ; }
}
```

7 Press **Start** or **F5** to run the application and see a text file written on your Desktop, or see an error message

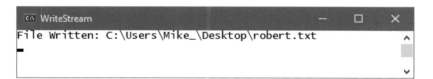

```
WriteStream                              —   □   ×
File Written: C:\Users\Mike_\Desktop\robert.txt
```

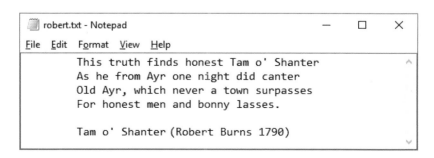

```
robert.txt - Notepad                      —   □   ×
File  Edit  Format  View  Help
          This truth finds honest Tam o' Shanter
          As he from Ayr one night did canter
          Old Ayr, which never a town surpasses
          For honest men and bonny lasses.

          Tam o' Shanter (Robert Burns 1790)
```

Hot tip

Try writing this file into a read-only directory to see an "Access to path denied" message.

Manipulating input and output

The **System.IO.**StreamReader class provides object methods that can be used to read text from a file. An instance of a StreamReader object must first be created using the **new** keyword, and the text file path specified as an argument to its "constructor":

StreamReader *name* = new StreamReader(*path*) ;

Methods such as **Read( )** and **ReadLine( )** can then be dot-suffixed to the object name. A StreamReader object is disposable, so its operation statements are best enclosed within a **using** construct to ensure it is removed from memory when the operation has completed. The **using** construct can also be wrapped in a **try-catch** block, to ensure the text file was read successfully.

Text read by a StreamReader object can be manipulated to change its format before output, for example, to manipulate cells exported from an Excel spreadsheet as comma-separated values:

Rank	Title	Artist
1	Can't Stop The Feeling	Justin Timberlake
2	One Dance	Drake
3	This Is What You Came For	Calvin Harris
4	Don't Let Me Down	The Chainsmokers
5	Cheap Thrills	Sia
	TopFive	

TopFive.csv - Notepad

File   Edit   Format   View   Help

```
Rank,Title,Artist
1,Can't Stop The Feeling,Justin Timberlake
2,One Dance,Drake
3,This Is What You Came For,Calvin Harris
4,Don't Let Me Down,The Chainsmokers
5,Cheap Thrills,Sia
```

ReadStream

1 Start a new **Console Application**, then name the project and Console.**Title** as "ReadStream"

2 Type this directive above the **namespace** declaration to make a further class library available to the program
using System.IO ;

3 Back in the **Main( )** method, add a statement to initialize a variable – insert your own user name in the path
string path = "C:\\Users*username*\\Desktop\\TopFive.csv" ;

4 Next, add a statement to display a message if the file cannot be read successfully

```
try
{
  // Statements to be inserted here (Step 5).
}
catch( Exception error )
{ Console.WriteLine( error.Message ) ; }
Console.ReadKey( ) ;
```

5 Now, insert statements that attempt to read the contents of the text file into a variable, line by line

```
using ( StreamReader reader = new StreamReader( path ) )
{
  string line ;
  while(  ( line = reader.ReadLine( )  ) != null )
  {
    // Statements to be inserted here (Steps 6-7).
  }
}
```

Hot tip

When the **ReadLine( )** method reaches the end of the file being read, it returns a **null** value.

6 Insert statements to modify the case of the column headers and amend an artist name

```
if( line.IndexOf( "Rank" ) != -1 ) line = line.ToUpper( ) ;
if( line.IndexOf( "Sia" ) != -1 ) line += " ft.Sean Paul" ;
```

7 Finally insert statements that display the content of just two columns, formatted for alignment

```
string [ ] sub = line.Split( ',' ) ;
line = String.Format( "{0,-30}{1,-20}", sub[1], sub[2] ) ;
Console.WriteLine( line ) ;
```

Hot tip

The String.**Format( )** placeholders specify character widths as negative numbers to align strings to the left.

8 Press **Start** or **F5** to run the application and see the manipulated output from the file content

```
ReadStream                                              —    □    ×
TITLE                         ARTIST
Can't Stop The Feeling        Justin Timberlake
One Dance                     Drake
This Is What You Came For     Calvin Harris
Don't Let Me Down             The Chainsmokers
Cheap Thrills                 Sia ft.Sean Paul
```

Summary

- The **System.IO** class is not automatically listed in the **using** directives generated by Visual Studio, so it must be added manually with a **using System.IO ;** statement.

- The **System.IO**.File class provides methods to easily read or write text files on your computer.

- The **System.IO**.File.**WriteAllText( )** method requires two arguments, to specify a file path and content to write there.

- The **System.IO**.File.**Exists( )** method will determine if the file specified as its argument already exists.

- It is recommended all read or write operations be wrapped in a **try-catch** block to report when an attempted operation fails.

- The **System.IO**.File.**WriteAllLines( )** method can write the element content of a **string** array as separate lines of a file.

- The **System.IO**.File.**AppendAllText( )** method requires two arguments to specify a file path and content to append there.

- The **System.IO**.File.**ReadAllText( )** method can be used to assign the entire content of a text file to a **string** variable.

- The **System.IO**.File.**ReadAllLines( )** method can assign individual lines of a text file to elements of a **string** array.

- The **System.IO**.StreamWriter class provides object methods to write text files on your computer.

- The **System.IO**.StreamReader class provides object methods to read from text files on your computer.

- An instance of a StreamReader object or StreamWriter object is created using the **new** keyword and by specifying a file path within the parentheses of its constructor.

- A StreamReader object has **Read( )** and **ReadLine( )** methods that can be dot-suffixed to an instance name.

- A StreamWriter object has **Write( )** and **WriteLine( )** methods that can be dot-suffixed to an instance name.

- All StreamReader and StreamWriter objects are disposable, so should each be enclosed in a **using** construct.

8 Solving problems

This chapter demonstrates how to detect and manage errors in C# programs.

Detecting real-time errors

As you type code in the **Code Editor** window, the Visual Studio IDE is constantly monitoring your code for possible errors. It examines the code you type, and provides real-time feedback of possible errors by adding a wavy underline to questionable code.

Warnings of potential problems are indicated by a green wavy underline. These are not critical and will not prevent execution of the application. A rollover tooltip explains the warning:

1 First, type this variable declaration in the **Code Editor**
int num

2 A green wavy line appears below the **num** variable name. Place the cursor over the green wavy underline to discover that the warning is merely indicating a potential problem as the variable has not yet been assigned a value

```
class Program
{
    static void Main(string[] args)
    {
        int num

            (local variable) int num

            The variable 'num' is declared but never used
    }
}
```

Errors are indicated by a red wavy underline. Unlike warnings, these are critical and will prevent execution of the application:

1 Next, type this variable declaration in the **Code Editor**
int num =

2 Place the cursor over the red wavy underline to discover that the error is due to a missing value in the expression

```
class Program
{
    static void Main(string[] args)
    {
        int num =

            Invalid expression term '}'

            ; expected
    }
}
```

Beware

Warnings can be ignored but errors must be corrected.

Real-time error detection in the Visual Studio IDE is a fantastic tool to help prevent errors when you are writing code. It not only indicates errors, but can even provide a list of correction options:

① Now, type this variable declaration in the **Code Editor**
`intr num = 1 ;`

Visual Studio 2019 provides live code analysis, which displays a light bulb when the compiler detects an issue with your code, and has a suggestion of how to fix that issue.

② A red wavy line appears below the **intr** variable type. Place the cursor over the red wavy underline to discover that the error is due to an unknown type specification

```
class Program
{
    static void Main(string[] args)
    {
        intr num = 1;

        ‍💡 ▾    The type or namespace name 'intr' could not be found
}           (are you missing a using directive or an assembly reference?)
}           Show potential fixes (Ctrl+.)
```

Other correction options allow you to create a new data type if that is what you require.

③ Click the light bulb icon, or click the **Show potential fixes** link, to see a list of error correction options

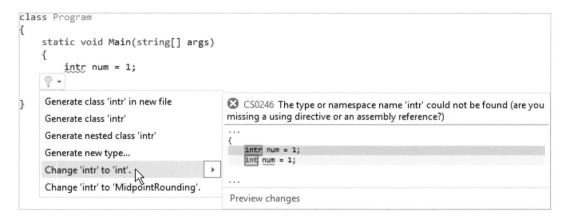

```
class Program
{
    static void Main(string[] args)
    {
        intr num = 1;

        💡 ▾
}
```

| Generate class 'intr' in new file |
| Generate class 'intr' |
| Generate nested class 'intr' |
| Generate new type... |
| Change 'intr' to 'int'. ▸ |
| Change 'intr' to 'MidpointRounding'. |

❌ CS0246 The type or namespace name 'intr' could not be found (are you missing a using directive or an assembly reference?)

```
...
{
    intr num = 1;
    int num = 1;
...
```

Preview changes

④ If this error is simply a spelling error for the **int** data type, select the option to **Change 'intr' to 'int'** – see your code get instantly corrected accordingly

Fixing compile-time errors

While syntax errors like those on page 99 can be detected by the **Code Editor** in real time, other errors that employ correct syntax cannot be detected until the code is compiled. Compile errors are typically errors of logic, and they cause the execution to halt when an "exception" occurs. For example, when incompatible data types appear in an expression, an **InvalidCastException** occurs and execution stops immediately:

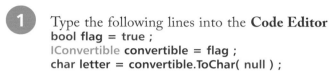

① Type the following lines into the **Code Editor**
```
bool flag = true ;
IConvertible convertible = flag ;
char letter = convertible.ToChar( null ) ;
```

② Press **Start** or **F5** to run the application and see execution is soon halted. The line causing the exception becomes highlighted in the **Code Editor** and an **Exception Assistant** pop-up window appears with a list of possible solutions

To fix this **InvalidCastException**, the code would need amending so both values are of compatible data types.

The cause of other compile errors may be less obvious without some further investigation. For example, when a loop that is reading array elements attempts to address an element index that does not exist, causing an **IndexOutOfRangeException**.

The **IConvertible** interface provides methods that convert a value to a CLR type, but it cannot meaningfully convert a **bool** to **char**.

You can click on the **View Detail** link for more error information.

100

...cont'd

Execution halts immediately, so it is useful to examine the counter value to identify the precise iteration causing the compile error.

1 In the **Code Editor**, type the following variable array declaration of 10 elements (0-9), and a loop
```
int [ ] nums = new int [ 10 ] ;
for ( int i = 1 ; i < 20 ; i++ ) { nums [ i ] = i ; }
```

2 Press **Start** or **F5** to run the application and see execution is soon halted. The code causing the exception becomes highlighted in the **Code Editor**, and an **Exception Assistant** pop-up window appears with a list of possible solutions

```
static void Main(string[] args)
{
    int[ ] nums = new int[ 10 ] ;
    for( int i = 1; i < 20; i++ ) { nums[i] = i ; }  ⊗
}
```
```
Exception Unhandled                                        ⇗ ✕

System.IndexOutOfRangeException: 'Index was outside the bounds of
the array.'


View Details │ Copy Details
```

3 Place the cursor over the assignment to the array variable to see a pop-up appear displaying its current value

```
static void Main(string[] args)
{

    int[ ] nums = new int[ 10 ] ;
    for( int i = 1; i < 20; i++ ) { nums[i] = i ; }  ⊗
}                                      ● i 10 ⇥
```

Beware

Another common compile error is the **FileNotFoundException** that occurs when a file is missing or its path name is incorrect.

It's now clear that execution halted when the loop attempted to address **nums[10]** – beyond the bounds of last element **nums[9]**. To fix this **IndexOutOfRangeException**, the code would need amending to end the loop after 10 iterations.

Debugging code

It is sometimes useful to closely examine the progression of a program by watching its execution line by line to locate any bugs. Progress is controlled by clicking the **Step Into** button on the **Debug** Menu Bar to move through the program one line at a time. When you begin debugging you can open a **Watch** window to monitor the value of particular variables as execution proceeds:

Debug

1 Add the following code within the **Main( )** method
```
int pass = 0 ;
int unit = 2 ;

for ( int i = 1 ; i < 3 ; i++ )
{
  pass = ( pass + 1 ) ;
  unit = square( unit ) ;
}
```

2 Now, add this arithmetic method after the **Main( )** method
```
static int square( int num )
{
  return ( num * num ) ;
}
```

3 In the **Code Editor,** click in the gray margin against the **Main( )** method – to set a debug starting "breakpoint"

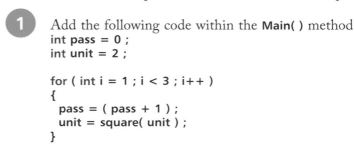

4 Click the **Step Into** button once to begin debugging

5 Click **Debug, Windows, Watch, Watch1** on the Menu Bar to launch a **Watch** window

6 Type the variable name "pass" into the **Name** column and hit **Enter,** then repeat to add the "unit" variable name

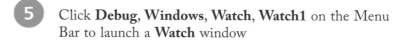

Name	Value	Type
pass	0	int
unit	0	int

Hot tip

If you can't see the **Step Into** button, right-click on the Menu Bar and select **Debug** to add the debugging buttons.

Don't forget

You can click the **Stop Debugging** button at any time to return to **Code Editor** mode.

7 Click **Step Into** seven times to reach the **square( )** method call in the first loop iteration, and note the values

```
for (int i = 1; i < 3; i++)
{
    pass = (pass + 1);
    unit = square(unit);
}
```

Watch 1		▾ □ ×
Name	Value	Type
🔘 pass	1	int
⬤ unit	2	int

8 Click **Step Into** 10 more times to progress through each line of the **square( )** method and the loop, returning to the **square( )** method call on the second iteration

```
for (int i = 1; i < 3; i++)
{
    pass = (pass + 1);
    unit = square(unit);
}
```

Watch 1		▾ □ ×
Name	Value	Type
🔘 pass	2	int
🔷 unit	4	int

9 Click the ↷ **Step Over** button once to execute the function without stepping through each line

```
for (int i = 1; i < 3; i++)
{
    pass = (pass + 1);
    unit = square(unit);
}
```

Watch 1		▾ □ ×
Name	Value	Type
🔘 pass	2	int
⬤ unit	16	int

10 Click the **Step Over** button four more times to move through to the end of the program

11 The debugger will automatically close and return to the regular **Code Editor** mode

12 Click the red dot you added in the margin to remove the breakpoint

Hot tip

The **Step Out** button is used to return to the function caller when you are stepping through lines of a called function.

Setting breakpoints

In all but the smallest of programs, stepping through each line is very tedious when debugging. Instead, you can quickly reach the part you wish to examine by setting multiple breakpoints to halt execution on particular lines. Setting one or more breakpoints is useful to help you understand how certain C# code constructs work – such as the nested loop construct shown here:

Breakpoints

1 Type this code to create three nested loops that each increment a counter variable within each loop, and a total pass iteration counter in the innermost loop

```csharp
int i , j , k ;
int pass = 0 ;

for ( i = 1 ; i < 4 ; i++ )
{
  for ( j = 1 ; j < 4 ; j++ )
  {
    for ( k = 1 ; k < 4 ; k++ )
    {
      pass++ ;
    }
  }
}
```

2 Click in the gray margin against each line containing the closing brace of each loop to set three breakpoints – a red dot will appear in the margin and each closing brace is highlighted to indicate the breakpoints are set

3 Click the **Start** button and see the application run to the first breakpoint it meets

Hot tip

Yellow arrows indicate the current position. Click on the red dot to cancel a breakpoint.

4 Click **Debug**, **Windows**, **Locals** to launch the **Locals** window and notice the current value of each variable

Locals			▼ □ ×
Name	Value	Type	
args	{string[0]}	string[]	
i	1	int	
j	1	int	
k	1	int	
pass	1	int	

5 Watch the variable values change as you repeatedly click the **Start** (**Continue**) button to move to each successive breakpoint until you reach the third outer loop breakpoint

6 Repeatedly click **Step Into** until you reach the closing brace of the **Main( )** method to see the final values

The **Locals** window shows all variables in current scope as the program proceeds.

```
20                          pass++;
21                      }
22                  }
23              }
24          }
```

Locals			▼ □ ×
Name	Value	Type	
args	{string[0]}	string[]	
i	4	int	
j	4	int	
k	4	int	
pass	27	int	

At the end of the program, each counter variable has been incremented beyond the upper limit set in the **for** statements, to exit each loop, and there has been a total of 27 iterations (3x3x3).

7 Click the **Start** button once more to run to the first breakpoint, then click **Debug**, **Windows**, **Immediate** to launch the **Immediate** window

8 In the **Immediate** window, type i = 3 and hit **Enter**, then use the **Step Into** button to step through each line of just the final complete outer loop's nine iterations

Any code you type into the **Immediate** window is dynamically applied to the application being debugged, but does not change its code.

Catching runtime errors

When you are able to predict potential runtime errors, by considering all eventualities, you can provide code to handle each Exception class error that may arise – by adding a **try-catch** construct. Your program can supply information to the user about the error, should you wish to do so, then proceed normally:

ErrorHandling

1 Add this program code to request user input of two numeric values for addition, then display their sum total

```
Console.Write( "Please Enter A Number: " ) ;
double num1 = Convert.ToInt16( Console.ReadLine( ) ) ;

Console.Write( "Now Enter Another Number: " ) ;
double num2 = Convert.ToInt16( Console.ReadLine( ) ) ;

Console.WriteLine( "Total: " + ( num1 + num2 ) ) ;
```

2 Press **Start** or **F5** to run the application, then enter any six-figure integer and hit **Enter**

```
ErrorHandling                                    —   □   ×
Please Enter A Number: 123456
```

3 The compiler reports an **OverflowException** error

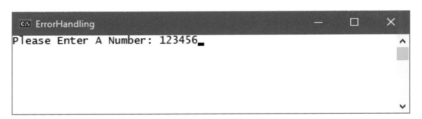

An Int16 is a 16-bit integer within the range -32,768 to +32,767 – whereas an Int32 is a 32-bit integer within -2,147,483,648 to +2,147,483,647.

4 Click the **Stop Debugging** button so you can edit the code

...cont'd

5 Drag the mouse to highlight all statements in Step 1, then right-click on the highlighted area and choose **Snippet**, **Insert Snippet:**, **Visual C#**, **try**

Insert Snippet: Visual C# |

- propfull
- propg
- sim
- struct
- svm
- switch
- try
- tryf
- unchecked

Hot tip

The **Insert Snippet** feature provides lots of useful pieces of code to paste into the **Code Editor** – take some time to explore its contents.

6 A **try-catch** construct is added to the code, enclosing the highlighted statements within the **try** block

7 Edit the default **catch** block to display an error message
`catch ( Exception error )`
`{ Console.WriteLine( error.Message ) ; }`

8 Run the application, then enter any six-figure integer and hit **Enter** to now see a default explanatory error message

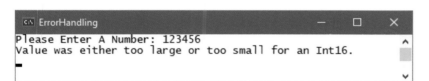

Hot tip

Each Exception has several methods and properties. For example, use **error.GetType()** to see the type of Exception.

You can provide your own error messages to handle a specific Exception by stating its type in the **catch( )** parentheses:

9 Edit the default **catch** block to display a custom message
`catch ( OverflowException )`
`{ Console.WriteLine( "\nMaximum: " + Int16.MaxValue ) ; }`

10 Run the application, then enter any six-figure integer and hit **Enter** to now see a custom explanatory error message

Hot tip

You can add multiple **catch** blocks after the **try** block, to handle different types of Exception.

The **Help Viewer** may not be installed by default when you install Visual Studio unless you select it from the Individual components list.

Getting help

The Visual Studio **Help** system provides an extensive source of reference for many programming languages. You can choose to install a Help library on your computer for the C# programming language so you can easily refer to it at any time, but the Help Viewer must first be installed in Visual Studio:

1 Click **Visual Studio Installer** on the Windows Start menu, then select the **Installed** menu item and click the **Modify** button on the Installer dialog

2 Select the **Individual components** tab, check the **Help Viewer** option, then click the **Modify** button to install the Help Viewer

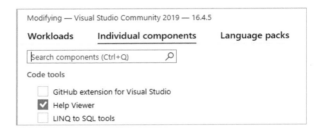

3 On the Visual Studio Menu Bar, click **Help**, **Add and Remove Help Content** to open the **Help Viewer**

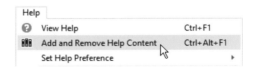

The **Help Viewer** allows you to download **Help** libraries for offline use, check for available updates, and seek help from installed **Help** libraries.

4 On the **Manage Content** tab, expand **Recommended Documentation**, then choose the **Add** link in the **Action** column for the **Visual C#** library

5 When your selection is added to the **Pending changes** list, click the **Update** button to download that library

You can **Set Help Preference** to **Launch in Browser** if you want to search online help without installing libraries, but local help is often more convenient.

6 On the Menu Bar, click **Help, Set Help Preference, Launch in Help Viewer** to use installed library

7 Next, click **Help, View Help** to launch **Help Viewer**

8 Now, select the **Index** tab in the left-hand pane

9 Type the item for help, such as "data types", in the **Help Viewer** Search box, then hit **Enter** to see the results

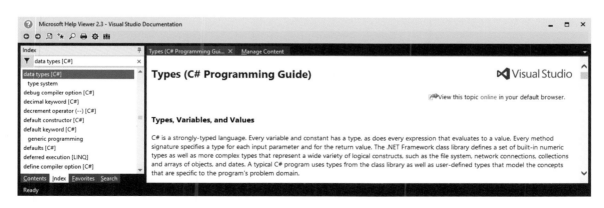

Summary

- The **Code Editor** constantly monitors your code to provide real-time error detection.

- Warnings are not critical and are indicated by a green wavy underline – whereas errors are critical and are indicated by a red wavy underline.

- A light bulb icon beside a red wavy underline indicates that a list of potential fixes is available.

- Typically, real-time errors are errors of syntax, and compile errors are errors of logic.

- When a compile error occurs in **Debug Mode**, execution stops and the **Exception Assistant** offers a list of possible fixes.

- In **Debug Mode** you can discover the current value of any variable simply by placing the cursor over the variable name.

- When debugging code, the **Step Into** button lets you walk through a program one line at a time.

- The **Step Over** button lets you bypass the lines of a called method, and the **Step Out** button lets you return to the line where that method is called.

- Variable values can be monitored as a program proceeds, using the **Watch** window or the **Locals** window.

- Breakpoints halt the execution of a program to allow examination of the part of the program where they are set.

- In **Debug Mode**, code can be dynamically applied using the **Immediate** window.

- Runtime errors occur when the user action has not been anticipated by the programmer.

- A **try-catch** block can be used to handle anticipated exceptions.

- The **Help** library system provides extensive reference sources for both offline and online assistance.

9 Creating objects

This chapter demonstrates encapsulation, inheritance, and polymorphism – the three principles of C# Object Oriented Programming.

Encapsulating data

A class is a data structure that can contain both variables and methods in a single entity. These are collectively known as its "members", and the variables are also known as its "properties".

If a class is not declared as **static** it can be used to create "instances" that are assigned to a variable for use by other classes.

Access to class members from outside the class is controlled by "access specifiers" in the **class** declaration. Typically, these will deny access to the variable members, but allow access to methods that can store and retrieve data from those variable members. This technique of "data hiding" ensures that stored data is safely encapsulated within the class variable members, and is the first principle of Object Oriented Programming (OOP).

A class declaration comprises a class access specifier, the **class** keyword, and a programmer-specified name – adhering to the usual C# naming conventions, but beginning in uppercase.

Don't forget

If not specified, the default access specifier for a class declaration is **internal**, and the default access specifier for class members is **private**.

The class declaration is followed by a pair of braces containing the variable and method declarations, which typically begin with their own access specifier. So, class syntax looks like this:

```
access-specifier class ClassName
{
  // Member variable property.
  access-specifier data-type variable-name ;

  // Member method.
  access-specifier return-type method-name ( parameter-list )
  {
    statements
  }
}
```

An access specifier may be any one of these keywords:

- **public** – accessible from any place where the class is visible
- **private** – accessible only to other members of the same class
- **protected** – accessible only to other members of the same class and members of classes derived from that class
- **internal** – accessible only to members of the same assembly

Hot tip

Derived classes, which use the **protected** member access specifier, are introduced later – see page 118.

112

...cont'd

Any real-world object can be defined by its attributes and by
its actions. For example, a dog has attributes such as name, age,
and color, plus actions it can perform such as bark. The class
mechanism in C# provides a way to create a virtual dog object
within a program, where the variable members of a class can
represent its attributes and the methods represent its actions:

```
public class Dog
{
  // MEMBER VARIABLES...
  private string name ;
  private int age ;
  private string color ;

  // MEMBER METHODS...

  // Setter & Getter Methods:
  public void setName( string tag )
  {
    name = tag ;          // Store the argument value.
  }

  public string getName( )
  {
    return name ;         // Retrieve the stored value.
  }

  public void setAge( int yrs ) { age = yrs ; }
  public int getAge( ) { return age ; }

  public void setColor( string coat ) { color = coat ; }
  public string getColor( ) { return color ; }

  // Other Methods:
  public string bark( ) { return "\nWoof, woof!\n" ; }
}
```

It is important to recognize that a class declaration only defines
a data structure – in order to create an object you must declare
an "instance" of that data structure, assigned to a variable. This
requires the **new** keyword and class name followed by parentheses:

```
// Create an instance named "fido" of the
// programmer-defined Dog data structure.
Dog fido = new Dog( ) ;
```

The principle of encapsulation in C# programming describes the
grouping together of data and functionality in class members
– name, age, color attributes, and bark action in the Dog class.

A program class cannot
perfectly emulate a real-
world object, but aims to
encapsulate all relevant
attributes and actions.

The **public** "setter" and
"getter" methods assign
values to, and retrieve
values from, the **private**
variable members.

It is conventional to
begin class names with
an uppercase character,
and object names with
lowercase.

Creating multiple objects

A program can easily create multiple objects simply by declaring multiple **new** instances of a **class**, and each object can have unique attributes by assigning individual values with its setter methods.

It is often convenient to combine the setter methods into a single method that accepts arguments for each **private** variable. This means that all values can be assigned with a single statement in the program, but the method will contain multiple statements.

In C# **class** declarations, the **public** "setter" methods, which assign data to **private** variable members, and **public** "getter" methods, which retrieve data from **private** variable members, are often named as the variable they address – but with the first letter made uppercase and prefixed by "set" or "get" respectively. For example, methods to access an **age** variable may be **setAge( )** and **getAge( )**.

Parameters may also be named as the variable they address. The code can differentiate between the parameter and like-named variable member by dot-prefixing **this** to the variable name:

Objects

Don't forget

In the setter method, the **this** prefixed names reference the **class** variable members, and those without prefix reference the parameters. No prefix is needed to reference the **class** variable members.

1 After the default Program **class**, declare a **class** named "Dog" with three variable members
```
public class Dog
{
  private string name , color ;
  private int age ;

  // Methods to be inserted here (Steps 2-4).
}
```

2 Next, insert a setter method for all variable members
```
public void setValues( string name, int age, string color )
{
  this.name = name ;
  this.age = age ;
  this.color = color ;
}
```

3 Now, insert getter methods for each variable member
```
public string getName( ) { return name ; }
public int getAge( ) { return age ; }
public string getColor( ) { return color ; }
```

4 Then, insert another miscellaneous method
```
public string bark( ) { return "\nWoof, woof!\n" ; }
```

...cont'd

5 Turn your attention to the **Main( )** method in the default **Program class** and create an instance of the **Dog** class
Dog fido = new Dog( ) ;

6 Next, call the new instance object's setter method to initialize all its variable members
fido.setValues("Fido" , 3 , "Brown") ;

7 Now, retrieve all properties of the new object
```
string tagF = String.Format( "{0} is a {1} year old {2} dog",
        fido.getName( ) ,
        fido.getAge( ) ,
        fido.getColor( )
) ;
```

8 Display all properties and call the miscellaneous method
Console.WriteLine(tagF + fido.bark( )) ;

9 Now, create another instance of the **Dog** class
Dog lucy = new Dog( ) ;
lucy.setValues("Lucy" , 2 , "Gray") ;

10 Next, retrieve all properties of this new object
```
string tagL = String.Format( "{0} is a {1} year old {2} dog",
        lucy.getName( ) ,
        lucy.getAge( ) ,
        lucy.getColor( )
) ;
```

11 Display all properties and call the miscellaneous method
Console.WriteLine(tagL + lucy.bark( )) ;
Console.ReadKey( ) ;

12 Press **Start** or **F5** to see each object's properties

Fido

Lucy

Hot tip

Notice here how the String.**Format( )** method call is coded using newlines to clearly build a **string** value for output.

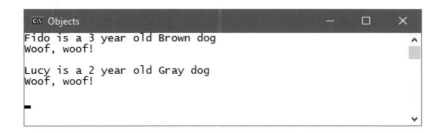

```
Objects                                      —   □   ×
Fido is a 3 year old Brown dog
Woof, woof!

Lucy is a 2 year old Gray dog
Woof, woof!
```

Initializing class members

Class variable members can be initialized by a special "constructor" method that is called whenever an instance of the class is created – allowing you to specify default values for class variable members.

The constructor method is always named exactly as the class name, and can contain statements to initialize class variable members. For example, **public class Cat** has a **public Cat( )** constructor.

When all class variables have been initialized by the class constructor method, any instance object of that class will immediately have those initial property values. Individual setter methods can usefully adjust the class variable values as needed:

Constructor

Don't forget

You cannot specify a constructor to be **private** as it must be accessible in order to create instance objects in other classes.

1 After the default Program **class**, declare a **class** named "Cat" with three variable members
```
public class Cat
{
  private string name , color ;
  private int age ;

  // Methods to be inserted here (Steps 2-5).
}
```

2 Next, insert a class constructor method to set default values for all its variable members
```
  public Cat( )
  {
    name = "Tigger" ;
    age = 3 ;
    color = "Brown" ;
  }
```

3 Now, insert setter methods for each variable member
```
public void setName( string name ) { this.name = name ; }
public void setAge( int age ) { this.age = age ; }
public void setColor( string color ) { this.color = color ; }
```

4 Then, insert getter methods for each variable member
```
public string getName( ) { return name ; }
public int getAge( ) { return age ; }
public string getColor( ) { return color ; }
```

5 Lastly, insert another miscellaneous class method
```
public string cry( ) { return "\nMeow, meow!\n" ; }
```

6 Turn your attention to the **Main( )** method in the default
Program **class** and create an instance of the Cat class
Cat **tigger = new** Cat( ) ;

7 Now, retrieve all (default) properties of the new object
string tagT = String.Format("{0} is a {1} year old {2} cat",
        tigger.getName( ) ,
        tigger.getAge( ) ,
        tigger.getColor( )
) ;

8 Display all properties and call the miscellaneous method
Console.**WriteLine(tagT + tigger.cry( )) ;**

9 Now, create another instance of the Cat class and set each
property with new values
Cat **smokey = new** Cat( ) ;

smokey.setName("Smokey") ;
smokey.setAge(2) ;
smokey.setColor("Gray") ;

10 Next, retrieve all (adjusted) properties of this new object
string tagS = String.Format("{0} is a {1} year old {2} cat",
        smokey.getName( ) ,
        smokey.getAge( ) ,
        smokey.getColor( )
) ;

11 Display all properties and call the miscellaneous method
Console.**WriteLine(tagS + smokey.cry( )) ;**
Console.**ReadKey( ) ;**

12 Press **Start** or **F5** to run the application and see the
properties of each object instance and method called

Tigger

Smokey

Hot tip

Object instances cannot
be created from **static**
classes, but you can
supply a constructor
method in **static** classes.

117

Hot tip

You can also specify
parameters to a
constructor method in
order to allow argument
values to be passed
when a **new** instance
object is created.

```
Constructor                              —    □    ×
Tigger is a 3 year old Brown cat
Meow, meow!

Smokey is a 2 year old Gray cat
Meow, meow!
```

Inheriting class properties

A C# class can be created as a brand new class, like those in previous examples, or can be "derived" from an existing class. Importantly, a derived class inherits members of the parent (base) class from which it is derived – in addition to its own members.

The ability to inherit members from a base class allows derived classes to be created that share certain common properties, which have been defined in the base class. For example, a "Polygon" base class may define width and height properties that are common to all polygons. Classes of "Rectangle" and Triangle" could be derived from the Polygon class – inheriting width and height properties, in addition to their own members defining their unique features.

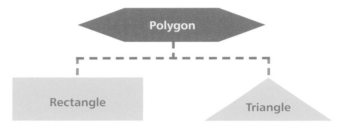

The virtue of inheritance is extremely powerful and is the second principle of Object Oriented Programming (OOP).

A derived class declaration adds a colon : after its class name, followed by the name of the class from which it derives:

Inheritance

1 After the default Program **class**, declare a base **class** named "Polygon", containing two variable members and one setter method member

```csharp
public class Polygon
{
  protected int width , height ;

  public void setValues( int width , int height )
  {
    this.width = width ;
    this.height = height ;
  }
}
```

...cont'd

2 Next, define a class that derives from the base class, inheriting members and adding a method

```
public class Rectangle : Polygon
{
  public int area( ) { return ( width * height ) ; }
}
```

3 Now, define another class that derives from the base class, inheriting members and adding a similar method to that in the previous step

```
public class Triangle : Polygon
{
  public int area( ) { return ( ( width * height ) / 2 ) ; }
}
```

4 Turn your attention to the **Main( )** method in the default Program **class** and create an instance object from each derived class

```
Rectangle rect = new Rectangle( ) ;
Triangle cone = new Triangle( ) ;
```

5 Call the inherited setter method of each derived class to initialize all the inherited variable members

```
rect.setValues( 4 , 5 ) ;
cone.setValues( 4 , 5 ) ;
```

6 Finally, call the added method in each derived class to display their computed values

```
Console.WriteLine( "Rectangle Area: " + rect.area( ) ) ;
Console.WriteLine( "\nTriangle Area: " + cone.area( ) ) ;
Console.ReadKey( ) ;
```

7 Press **Start** or **F5** to run the application and see the output from inherited variables

```
C# Inheritance                              —    □    ×
Rectangle Area: 20
Triangle Area: 10
```

Hot tip

The : operator is used here to create derived classes, and is equivalent to the **extends** keyword in other programming languages – such as Java.

Don't forget

The methods added to each derived class can be named alike, as they only exist within the scope of their respective class.

119

Don't forget

Notice that the setter method and variables are not defined in the derived classes, as they are inherited from the base class.

Calling base constructors

Although derived classes inherit the members of their parent base class, they do not inherit its constructor method. Nonetheless, a constructor method of the base class is always called when a new object of a derived class is created. The call to the base class constructor method is made in addition to the call to the constructor method of the derived class.

The default constructor method of a base class has no parameters – but the base class may also have one or more "overloaded" constructor methods that do have parameters.

If you prefer to call an overloaded constructor of the base class when a new object of a derived class is created, you can create a matching overloaded constructor in the derived class – having the same number and type of arguments. The matching derived class constructor must then explicitly call the overloaded base class constructor using the **base** keyword. This is appended to the derived class constructor declaration after a : colon character.

When a new object of a derived class is created, argument values can be passed to an overloaded derived class constructor, and also onwards to its matching overloaded base class constructor in parentheses following the **base** keyword:

Base

1   After the default Program **class**, declare a base **class** named "Parent", containing a default constructor method

```
public class Parent
{
  public Parent( )
  {
    Console.WriteLine( "Parent Called" ) ;
  }

  // Overloaded constructor to be inserted here (Step 2).
}
```

2   Next, insert an overloaded constructor method into the base class that requires a single integer argument

```
public Parent( int num )
{
    Console.WriteLine( "Parent+ Called: " + num ) ;
}
```

3 After the base class, add a derived class containing a default constructor method

```
public class Daughter : Parent
{
  public Daughter( )
  { Console.WriteLine( "\tDaughter Called\n" ) ; }
}
```

4 Next, add another derived class, containing a default constructor method

```
public class Son : Parent
{
  public Son( )
  { Console.WriteLine( "\tSon Called\n" ) ; }

  // Overloaded constructor to be inserted here (Step 5).
}
```

Son – Parent – Daughter

5 Now, insert an overloaded constructor method into the derived class, which requires a single integer argument

```
public Son( int num ) : base( num )
{
  Console.WriteLine( "\tSon+ Called: " + num ) ;
}
```

The default base constructor method will be called implicitly unless the **base** keyword is used to call explicitly.

6 Turn your attention to the **Main( )** method in the default Program **class** and create instances of the derived classes

```
Daughter anna = new Daughter( ) ;
Son brad = new Son( ) ;
Son carl = new Son( 100 ) ;
Console.ReadKey( ) ;
```

7 Press **Start** or **F5** to run the application and see the output from base and derived class constructors

```
CS Base                                        —    □    ×
Parent Called
        Daughter Called

Parent Called
        Son Called

Parent+ Called: 100
        Son+ Called: 100
```

Here, the argument value is passed to the derived class and base class.

Hiding base methods

A method can be declared in a derived class to "hide" a similar method in the base class – if both method declarations have matching name, arguments, and return type.

Creation of a matching method in a derived class effectively hides the base class method, as it generally becomes inaccessible. To indicate that hiding is intentional, rather than accidental, the hiding method declaration should include the **new** keyword.

Base class methods can be called explicitly from within non-static classes by prefixing their method name with the **base** keyword. Alternatively, as a derived class is a specialization of its base class, base class methods can be called explicitly using an explicit cast:

Hide

1 After the default Program **class**, declare a base **class** named "Man", containing a simple method without parameters plus an overloaded method with a single parameter

```
public class Man
{
  public void speak( )
  {
    Console.Write( "Hello: " ) ;
  }

  public void speak( string message )
  {
    Console.WriteLine( message + "!\n" ) ;
  }
}
```

Don't forget

A derived class method name and parameter list must match that in its base class to override it.

2 After the base class, add a derived class containing a method to intentionally hide the overloaded method of the same name and parameters in the base class

```
public class Hombre : Man
{
  public new void speak( string message )
  {
    // Statement to be inserted here (Step 3).
    Console.WriteLine( message ) ; }
}
```

3 Next, insert a statement in the derived class to explicitly call the simple method in the base class

```
  base.speak( ) ;
```

4 Turn your attention to the **Main( )** method in the default
Program **class**, and create an instance of the base class
Man **henry = new** Man**( ) ;**

5 Next, create an instance of the derived class
Hombre **enrique = new** Hombre**( ) ;**

Henry   Enrique

6 Add a call to the simple method inherited by the instance
from the base class
henry.speak( ) ;

7 Now, add a call to the overloaded method inherited from
the base class
henry.speak("It's a beautiful evening" **) ;**

8 Then, add a call to the hiding method in the derived class
– that will also explicitly call the simple method in the
base class
enrique.speak("Hola..." **) ;**

The **base** keyword
cannot be used in the
Main( ) method, as that
is a **static** method.

9 Finally, add a statement using an explicit cast – to
explicitly call the overloaded method in the base class
((Man**) enrique).speak(** "Es una tarde hermosa" **) ;**
Console**.ReadKey( ) ;**

10 Press **Start** or **F5** to run the application and see the
output from base class methods and hiding method

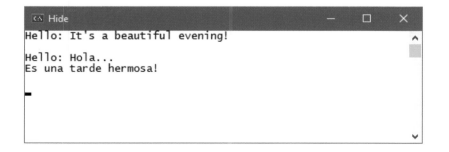

123

Directing method calls

The three cornerstones of Object Oriented Programming (OOP) are **encapsulation**, **inheritance**, and **polymorphism**. Previous examples have demonstrated **encapsulation** of data within a class, and **inheritance** of base class members by derived classes. The term **polymorphism** (from Greek, meaning "many forms") describes the ability to assign a different meaning or purpose to an entity according to its context. C# overloaded operators can be described as polymorphic. For example, the + symbol represents the addition or concatenation operator – according to its context. C# class methods can also be polymorphic. Method declarations in a base class can include the **virtual** keyword to allow that method to be overridden in derived classes. Similarly, method definitions in a derived class can include the **override** keyword to denote it will be overriding a **virtual** base class method. In this way, derived class methods can provide their own version of a base class method. The great advantage of polymorphism with multiple derived class objects is that calls to methods of the same name are directed to the appropriate overriding method. This can allow inconsistencies, however – this example seems to imply that chickens can fly!

Override

1 After the default Program **class**, declare a base **class** named "Bird", containing two methods that allow overriding
```
public class Bird
{
  public virtual void talk( )
  { Console.WriteLine( "A Bird Talks..." ) ; }

  public virtual void fly( )
  { Console.WriteLine( "A Bird Flies...\n" ) ; }
}
```

Here, the **fly( )** method in each derived class also calls the base class **fly( )** method directly.

2 After the base class, add a derived class containing two methods that will override the base class methods
```
public class Pigeon : Bird
{
  public override void talk( )
  { Console.WriteLine( "Pigeon Says: Coo! Coo!" ) ; }

  public override void fly( )
  {
    Console.WriteLine( "A Pigeon Flies Away..." ) ;
    base.fly( ) ;
  }
}
```

3 Next, add another derived class containing two methods that will also override the base class methods

```csharp
public class Chicken : Bird
{
  public override void talk( )
  { Console.WriteLine( "Chicken Says: Cluck! Cluck!" ) ; }

  public override void fly( )
  {
    Console.WriteLine( "I'm A Chicken - I Can't Fly" ) ;
    base.fly( ) ;
  }
}
```

Beware

You must use the **base** keyword prefix to directly call a base class method from a derived class.

4 Turn your attention to the default Program **class** and add a method to call both overriding methods

```csharp
static void describe( Bird obj )
{
  obj.talk( ) ;
  obj.fly( ) ;
}
```

Hot tip

Each instance object is passed as an argument for C# to determine the appropriate overriding method to execute.

5 Turn your attention to the **Main( )** method in the default Program **class** and create instances of each non-base class

```csharp
Pigeon joey = new Pigeon( ) ;
Chicken lola = new Chicken( ) ;
```

6 Finally, add statements to call appropriate methods

```csharp
describe( joey ) ;
describe( lola ) ;
Console.ReadKey( ) ;
```

7 Press **Start** or **F5** to run the application and see the output from overriding methods and base class method

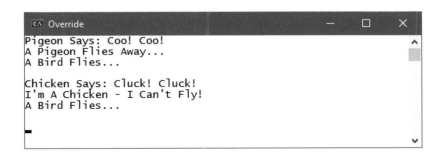

Hot tip

Polymorphism in programming is often called "one interface, multiple functions".

Providing capability classes

Classes whose sole purpose is to allow other classes to be derived from them are known as "capability classes" – they provide capabilities to the derived classes. Capability classes generally contain no data, but merely declare a number of methods that can be overridden in their derived classes.

A capability class and its methods can all be declared using the **abstract** keyword to denote that they can only be implemented in derived classes. In this case, the method signature is followed by a semicolon, rather than a method block containing statements. Method definitions in derived classes can then include the **override** keyword to implement the capability class methods.

Adding the **sealed** keyword to a class declaration is a safeguard that prevents that class being used as a base class. Understandably, an **abstract** capability class cannot be **sealed**.

The following example builds upon the previous example on pages 124-125 to demonstrate how the "Bird" class can be better written as a capability class. This now prevents the base class methods being called directly, to avoid inconsistencies:

You cannot create an instance of an **abstract** base class.

Capability

1 After the default `Program` **class**, define a base capability **class** named "Bird", containing two methods
```
public abstract class Bird
{
  public abstract void talk( ) ;

  public abstract void fly( ) ;
}
```

2 Add a derived class containing two methods that will override the base class methods
```
public sealed class Pigeon : Bird
{
  public override void talk( )
  { Console.WriteLine( "Pigeon Says: Coo! Coo!" ) ; }

  public override void fly( )
  { Console.WriteLine( "A Pigeon Flies Away..." ) ; }
}
```

...cont'd

3 Next, add another class that also contains two methods that will override the base class methods
```
public sealed class Chicken : Bird
{
  public override void talk( )
  { Console.WriteLine( "Chicken Says: Cluck! Cluck!" ) ; }

  public override void fly( )
  { Console.WriteLine( "I'm A Chicken - I Can't Fly" ) ; }
}
```

Chicken   Pigeon
(Bird)   (Bird)

4 Next, add another class containing a single method that accepts an object argument
```
public sealed class Caller
{
  public void describe( Bird obj )
  {
    obj.talk( ) ;
    obj.fly( ) ;
  }
}
```

5 Turn your attention to the **Main( )** method in the default Program **class** and create instances of each non-base class
```
Pigeon joey = new Pigeon( ) ;
Chicken lola = new Chicken( ) ;
Caller call = new Caller( ) ;
```

6 Finally, add statements to call appropriate methods by passing an object as an argument
```
call.describe( joey ) ;
call.describe( lola ) ;
Console.ReadKey( ) ;
```

7 Press **Start** or **F5** to run the application and see the output from the overriding methods of derived classes

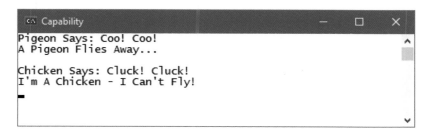

```
Pigeon Says: Coo! Coo!
A Pigeon Flies Away...

Chicken Says: Cluck! Cluck!
I'm A Chicken - I Can't Fly!
```

Each instance object is passed as an argument for C# to determine the appropriate overriding method to execute.

Employing partial classes

The source code for each example listed in this book is generally contained in a single **.cs** file, as each one is just a simple program. When working on larger projects it is often desirable to spread the source code over separate files to allow multiple programmers to work on the project at the same time. Visual Studio allows you to easily add one or more code files in which to write classes.

Class definitions can also be spread across several files by including the **partial** keyword in each separate part of the definition. Providing all parts have the same level of accessibility, the C# compiler will combine all parts into a single definition:

Beware

If any part is declared **abstract**, the whole class will be **abstract**, and if any part is declared **sealed**, the whole class will be **sealed**.

Parts

128

Hot tip

Alternatively, you can right-click on the project name in Solution Explorer and choose **Add**, **New Item** to launch this dialog box.

1 Start a new **Console Application**, then name the project and Console.**Title** as "Parts"

2 From the Visual Studio menu, select **Project**, **Add Class** to launch the "Add New Item" dialog box

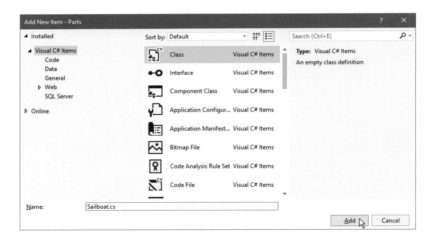

3 Edit the name field to the name of the class to be added there – in this case, it's to be a **class** named "Sailboat"

4 Click the **Add** button to add the new file to your project

5 Next, select **View, Solution Explorer** and click on **Sailboat.cs** to open that file in the **Code Editor**

6 Edit the added file to provide a class constructor part

```
public partial class Sailboat
{
  private string make ;
  private string model ;

  public Sailboat( string make , string model )
  {
    this.make = make ;
    this.model = model ;
  }
}
```

Laser
Sailboat (Boat)

7 Now, in **Solution Explorer**, click on **Program.cs** to open that file in the **Code Editor**

8 After the default Program **class** add a class method part

```
public partial class Sailboat
{
  public void describe( )
  {
    Console.WriteLine( "Sailboat: {0} {1}" , make , model ) ;
  }
}
```

Notice how the strings are substituted for output in this example.

129

9 Turn your attention to the **Main( )** method in the default Program **class** and create an instance object

```
Sailboat boat = new Sailboat( "Laser" , "Classic" ) ;
```

10 Finally, add a statement to call the added class method

```
boat.describe( ) ;
Console.ReadKey( ) ;
```

Partial classes are part of the same **namespace** – here, it is "Parts".

11 Press **Start** or **F5** to run the application and see the output from the class parts spread over two files

```
Parts                                    —    □    ×
Sailboat: Laser Classic
```

Summary

- Encapsulation, inheritance, and polymorphism are the three cornerstones of Object Oriented Programming.

- A C# **class** is a data structure that can contain both variable members and method members.

- Access to **class** members is controlled by access specifiers.

- An instance object of a **class** is created using the **new** keyword followed by the class name and parentheses.

- Typically, **public** setter and getter methods provide access to **private** variables to ensure stored data is safely encapsulated.

- Parameters can be named as the variable they address, and the **this** keyword prefix can be used to differentiate between them.

- The constructor method of a **class** is named as the class name and is called each time an instance of that **class** is created.

- Derived classes inherit members of the base parent **class** from which they are derived.

- A derived **class** declaration adds a colon after the class name, followed by the name of the **class** from which it derives.

- An overloaded constructor of a base **class** can be called using the **base** keyword in a derived class declaration.

- A derived **class** can include a **new** method to hide a method in its parent class if name, arguments, and return type match.

- Base class methods can be called explicitly from a derived class by prefixing the method name with the **base** keyword.

- The **virtual** and **override** keywords can be used to allow base class methods to be overridden by derived class methods.

- Capability classes can include the **abstract** keyword to denote their methods can only be implemented in derived classes.

- Adding the **sealed** keyword to a class declaration is a safeguard that prevents that class being used as a base class.

- Class definitions can be spread across several files by including the **partial** keyword in each part of the definition.

10 Controlling events

This chapter demonstrates how a C# program can recognize and respond to events that occur in a graphical application.

Starting a Forms project

Visual Studio provides a **Windows Forms Application** template that allows you to easily create a C# program that provides a Graphical User Interface (GUI) to interact with the user:

FirstGUI

1 On the Menu Bar, click **File**, **New**, **Project**, to open the "Create a new project" dialog

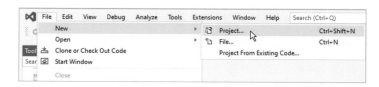

Hot tip

Windows GUI applications provide interactive controls that produce "events" in response to user actions, and your program can respond to those actions. This is known as event-driven programming.

2 In the "Create a new project" dialog, select **Windows Forms App (.NET Framework)** then click **Next**

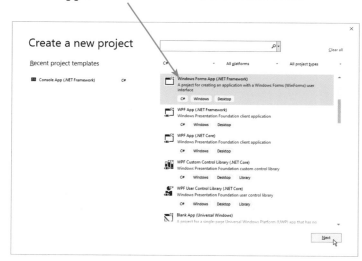

3 Enter a project name of your choice in the **Name** field, then click on the **Create** button to create the new project – in this case, the project name will be "FirstGUI"

Hot tip

You can open the FormDesigner window from the menu by clicking **View**, **Designer** or by pressing the **F7** keyboard key.

4 Wait while Visual Studio creates your new project and loads it into the IDE, then you should see a **Form Designer** window appear displaying an empty Form

5 Select the **View, Solution Explorer** menu to open a Solution Explorer window and see all files in your project

132

6 Now, select the **View**, **Properties** menu to open a **Properties** window to reveal all properties of your Form

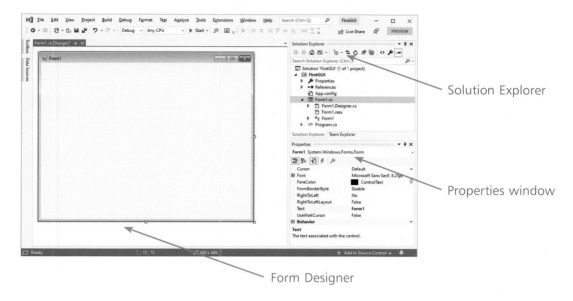

Solution Explorer

Properties window

Form Designer

The **Form Designer** is where you create visual interfaces for your applications, and the **Properties** window contains details of the item that is currently selected in the Form Designer window.

7 The Visual Studio IDE has now gathered all the resources needed to build a default Windows application – click the **Start** button on the toolbar to launch this application

The application simply creates a basic window – you can move it, minimize it, maximize it, resize it, and quit the application by closing it. It may not do much, but you have already created a real Windows GUI app!

Alternatively, you can run applications using the **Debug**, **Start Debugging** menu options or by pressing the **F5** keyboard key.

Adding visual controls

The **Toolbox** in the Visual Studio IDE contains a wide range of visual controls, which are the building blocks of your applications. Using the project created on pages 132-133, follow these steps to start using the Toolbox now:

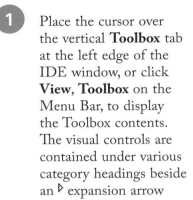

FirstGUI
(continued)

1 Place the cursor over the vertical **Toolbox** tab at the left edge of the IDE window, or click **View**, **Toolbox** on the Menu Bar, to display the Toolbox contents. The visual controls are contained under various category headings beside an ▷ expansion arrow

Any pinned Window in the IDE can be dragged from its usual location to any position you prefer. Drag back to the initial location to re-dock it.

2 Click on the expansion arrow beside the **Common Controls** category heading to expand the list of the most commonly used visual controls. Usefully, each control name appears beside an icon depicting that control as a reminder. You can click on the category heading again to collapse the list, then expand the other categories to explore the range of controls available to build your application interfaces

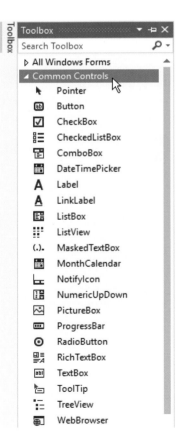

The **Toolbox** will automatically hide when you click on another part of the IDE, but it can be fixed in place so it will never hide, using the ⊞ **Pin** button on the Toolbox bar.

3 Click and drag the **Button** item from the Common Controls category in the Toolbox onto the Form in the Designer window, or double-click the Button item, to add a Button control to the Form

The Button control appears on the Form surrounded by "handles" that can be dragged to resize the button's width and height.

4 Click the ▶ **Start** button to run the application and see the Button control appear in its initial default state

5 Next, move the pointer over the Button control to see its appearance change to its "MouseHover" state

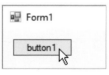

6 Now, click and hold down the Button control to see its appearance change to its "MouseDown" state

7 Finally, release the Button control to see its appearance change to its "MouseUp" state

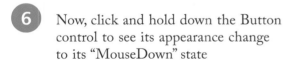

Each change of appearance is Windows' default response to an event that occurs on the Button control, but your C# program can provide its own response to these, and many more, control events:

8 Select the Button control then open its **Properties** window

9 Click the **Events** button and scroll down to see all possible Button events

135

Writing functional code

The Visual Studio IDE automatically generates code in the background, to incorporate the visual controls you add to your program interface. Additional code can be added manually to the "code-behind" page using the IDE's integral **Code Editor**, to determine how your program should respond to interface events:

Using the project created on pages 132-135, follow these steps to add your own responses to user actions that produce events:

Use the tabs to switch between the **Code Editor** and the **Form Designer**.

FirstGUI
(continued)

1 Select the Button control named **button1**, then open its **Properties** window and click the **Events** button

2 Double-click on the **MouseHover** item to open a **Form1.cs** code-behind page in the **Code Editor** at a generated event-handler method

3 Next, insert this statement within the generated method – to change the Button's background color in response to a **MouseHover** event
button1.BackColor = Color.Fuchsia ;

The Color class provides lots of standard color properties – type Color then a period and use IntelliSense to see them.

```csharp
Form1.cs    Form1.cs [Design]
C# FirstGUI                                              FirstGUI.Form1
    24
    25          private void button1_MouseHover(object sender, EventArgs e)
    26          {
    27              button1.BackColor = Color.Fuchsia;
    28          }
```

4 Similarly, double-click on the **MouseDown** item and insert this statement within another generated method – to change the Button's background color in response to a **MouseDown** event
button1.BackColor = Color.Lime ;

The lines of code in this example are to be inserted into each individual event-handler method that is automatically generated by Visual Studio.

5 Likewise, double-click on the **MouseUp** item and insert this statement within a further generated method – to change the Button's background color in response to a **MouseUp** event
button1.BackColor = Color.Aqua ;

6 Now, click the **Form1.cs [Design]** tab to return to the **Form Designer** window

7 Double-click on the Button control on the Form to open the **Form1.cs** code-behind page in the **Code Editor** at yet another generated event-handler method

8 Finally, insert this statement within the generated method – to open a message box in response to a **Click** event
MessageBox.**Show**("C# Programming in easy steps") ;

9 Run the application, then click the button to see the **MouseHover**, **MouseDown**, and **Click** event responses

You can use the **View** menu on the Menu Bar to open the **Code Editor**, the **Form Designer**, or any other window you require at any time.

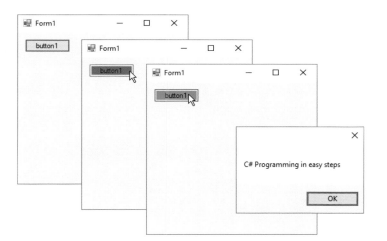

You can see many more uses for the MessageBox class on page 142.

10 Push the **OK** button to close the message box and see the **MouseUp** event response

Most Windows software works by responding to events. For example, when you press a key, a **KeyPress** event can call its event-handler to respond to that event.

Gathering text entries

A **Label** control is generally used to display non-dynamic text.

Entry

In the **Layout** property category, you must set **AutoSize** to **False** before you can adjust the **Width** and **Height** values in the **Size** property category.

A **TextBox** control can be added to a Form in a **Windows Forms Application** to allow the user to enter input. The current value within a **TextBox** can be assigned to a variable, typically in response to a **Button Click** event, for use inside the program code.

A new value can be assigned to a **TextBox** as output to the user, but the user can modify this value. Alternatively, output can be assigned to a **Label** control, which the user cannot modify:

1 Start a new **Windows Forms Application**, then add a **TextBox**, a **Button**, and two **Label** controls

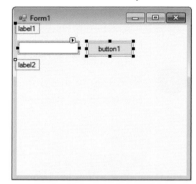

2 Select the Form itself, then in the **Properties** window modify its **Text** value and height

3 Next, modify the **Text** property values of the **Button** control and **Label** controls so they look like this:

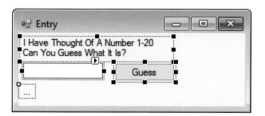

4 Now, double-click the **Button** control to open the **Code Editor** at a generated **Click** event-handler

5 At the very beginning of the **Form1** class block, add a variable with setter and getter methods
private int num ;
public void setNum(int num) { this.num = num ; }
public int getNum( ) { return num ; }

```
13    public partial class Form1 : Form
14    {
15        private int num;
16        public void setNum(int num) { this.num = num; }
17        public int getNum() { return num; }
```

6 In the **Form1( )** constructor method block, insert statements to initialize the variable with a random value
Random **rnd** = new Random( ) ;
setNum(rnd.Next(1, 21)) ;

```
19        public Form1()
20        {
21            InitializeComponent();
22            Random rnd = new Random();
23            setNum( rnd.Next(1, 21) );
24        }
```

Beware

If you specify minimum and maximum arguments to the **Next( )** method, it will return a random integer between the specified minimum and <u>maximum-1</u> – so specifying 21 will allow a maximum of 20.

7 Then, add a method to compare two arguments and set a Label control's Text property with an appropriate message
public void rate(int guess, int num)
{
  if (guess < num) label2.text = "Too Low!" ;
  else
  if (guess > num) label2.text = "Too High!" ;
  else
  label2.text = "*** Correct ***" ;
}

8 Finally, insert statements within the **Button Click** event-handler to compare user input against the random value
int guess = Convert.ToInt16(textBox1.text) ;
rate(guess, getNum( )) ;

```
35        private void button1_Click(object sender, EventArgs e)
36        {
37            int guess = Convert.ToInt16(textBox1.Text);
38            rate(guess, getNum());
39        }
```

Don't forget

The content of a **TextBox** control is a string value – so it must be converted to a numeric data type for numeric comparison.

9 Press **Start** or **F5** to run the application and enter input to see the appropriate output messages

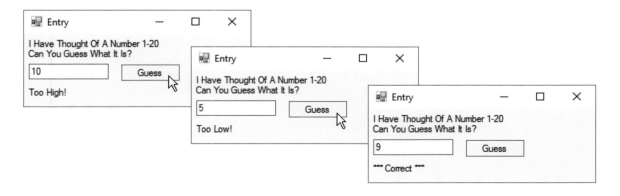

Ticking option boxes

A **CheckBox** control is a small box with a caption. It lets the user select the caption choice by clicking on the box, and a check mark appears in the box to indicate it has been chosen. Clicking the box once more deselects the choice and unchecks the box. **CheckBox** controls are ideal to present a set of choices from which the user can select none, one, or more than one choice.

A **RadioButton** control is like a **CheckBox**, but with one crucial difference – the user can check only one choice in the group. Checking a **RadioButton** automatically unchecks any others. **RadioButton** controls are ideal to present a set of choices from which the user can select only one choice.

Selected **CheckBox** and **RadioButton** items can usefully be added to the collection displayed in a **ListBox** control:

Hot tip

Set one **RadioButton** control to **Checked** to specify a default option.

Option

1 Start a new **Windows Forms Application**, then add **RadioButton**, **CheckBox**, **ListBox**, **Button**, and **Label** controls to the Form

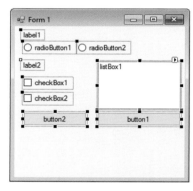

2 Modify the **Text** property values of the controls to look like this:

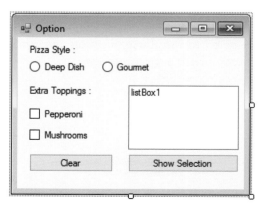

Don't forget

The name of the **ListBox** control that appears in the Form Designer will not be displayed when the application runs.

3 Now, double-click the "Show Selection" **Button** control to open the **Code Editor** at its generated **Click** event-handler

140

4 In the **Form1( )** constructor method block, insert a
statement to specify a default option
radioButton1.Checked = true ;

5 Next, insert a statement within the "Show Selection"
Button Click event-handler to empty any listed items
listBox1.Items.Clear( ) ;

6 Insert statements within the "Show Selection" **Button
Click** event-handler to add selected options to the list
```
if ( radioButton1.Checked )
  listBox1.Items.Add( radioButton1.Text ) ;
if ( radioButton2.Checked )
  listBox1.Items.Add( radioButton2.Text ) ;
if ( checkBox1.Checked )
  listBox1.Items.Add( checkBox1.Text ) ;
if ( checkBox2.Checked )
  listBox1.Items.Add( checkBox2.Text ) ;
```

The **ListBox** control has
an **Items** property that
provides methods to add
or remove list items from
a collection.

7 Now, double-click the "Clear" **Button** control to open the
Code Editor at its generated **Click** event-handler

8 Insert statements within the "Clear" **Button Click** event-
handler to reset all the options
```
listBox1.Items.Clear( ) ;
radioButton1.Checked = true ;
checkBox1.Checked = false ;
checkBox2.Checked = false ;
```

9 Press **Start** or **F5** to run the application and select
options to see them appear in the list – then hit **Clear**

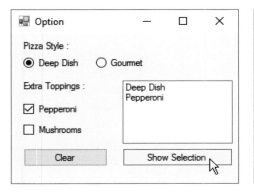

Showing user messages

The features of a MessageBox dialog can be determined by adding three further arguments after the message string within its **Show( )** method. These can specify a caption, which buttons the dialog will display, and which graphic icon will appear on the dialog.

A **MessageBox** is "modal" – the user must deal with its dialog message before the program can proceed.

142

MessageBoxButtons constants
AbortRetryIgnore
OK
OKCancel
RetryCancel
YesNo
YesNoCancel

The dialog button combinations can be specified using the MessageBoxButtons constant values listed in this table. For example, to have the dialog display Yes, No, and Cancel buttons, specify the MessageBoxButtons. **YesNoCancel** constant.

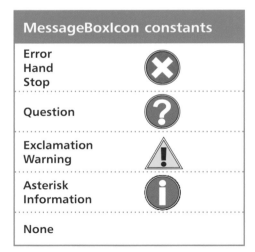

MessageBoxIcon constants	
Error Hand Stop	
Question	
Exclamation Warning	
Asterisk Information	
None	

The dialog icon can be specified using the MessageBoxIcon constant values listed in this table. For example, to have the dialog display the question mark icon, specify the MessageBoxIcon. **Question** constant.

Hot tip

Always specify a graphic icon when calling a **MessageBox** dialog to help the user easily understand the nature of the message.

When the user presses a MessageBox dialog button it returns an appropriate DialogResult constant value to the program. These are named exactly as the individual button label they represent. For example, any MessageBox dialog OK button returns the DialogResult.**OK** constant. The program can therefore examine the returned value to determine how to proceed.

1 Start a new **Windows Forms Application**, then add a **Button**, a **TextBox**, and a **Label** control to the Form

Message

2 Double-click the "Show Message" **Button** control to open the **Code Editor** at its generated **Click** event-handler

3 Insert a block within the "Show Message" **Button Click** event-handler to deliberately throw an exception

```
try
{
  throw new NotImplementedException( ) ;
}
catch ( NotImplementedException notImp )
{
  // Statements to be inserted here (Steps 4-5 ).
}
```

Hot tip

This technique of throwing a NotImplementedException is favored by some programmers as a reminder to complete an unfinished part of the program code.

143

4 Add a statement to assign the user's decision to a variable

```
DialogResult result =
MessageBox.Show( "Proceed?", notImp.Message ,
  MessageBoxButtons.YesNo , MessageBoxIcon.Error ) ;
```

5 Now, add statements to respond to the user's decision

```
textBox1.Text = result.ToString( ) ;
if( result == DialogResult.Yes ) label1.Text = "Proceeding..." ;
if( result == DialogResult.No ) label1.Text = "Stopping..." ;
```

6 Press **Start** or **F5** to run the application and use the **MessageBox** buttons to determine how to proceed

Hot tip

Alternatively, this program could stop by calling the form's **Close( )** method in response to DialogResult.**No**.

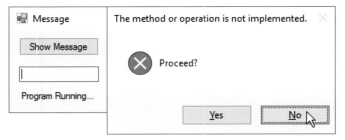

Calling system dialogs

Visual Studio makes it simple to add the ability to call upon the standard Windows selection dialogs so the user can choose options within your applications – for example, selection of colors, fonts, and images:

Dialog

1 Start a new **Windows Forms Application** project and add a **PictureBox**, a **TextBox**, and three **Button** controls to the Form

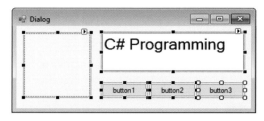

2 From the **Dialogs** section of the **Toolbox**, add a **ColorDialog**, a **FontDialog**, and an **OpenFileDialog** component to the Form – see them appear in the **Component Tray** at the bottom of the Form Designer

The **DialogResult.OK** value indicates the user pressed the OK button – just as it does in the **MessageBox** example on page 143.

3 Double-click the first **Button** to open the **Code Editor** at its generated **Click** event-handler, then insert this code to change the background color of the **Form**
```
if ( colorDialog1.ShowDialog( ) == DialogResult.OK )
  this.BackColor = colorDialog1.Color ;
```

4 Double-click the second **Button** to open the **Code Editor** at its generated **Click** event-handler, then insert this code to change the font of the **TextBox** control
```
if ( fontDialog1.ShowDialog( ) == DialogResult.OK )
  textBox1.Font = fontDialog1.Font ;
```

The **SaveFileDialog** is demonstrated in the example on page 149.

5 Double-click the third **Button** to open the **Code Editor** at its generated **Click** event-handler, then insert this code to choose an image for the **PictureBox** control
```
if ( openFileDialog1.ShowDialog( ) == DialogResult.OK )
{
  // Statements to be inserted here (Step 6).
}
```

6 Insert a block to assign a selected image or display an error message

```
try
{
  pictureBox1.SizeMode =
        PictureBoxSizeMode.StretchImage ;
  pictureBox1.Image =
        new Bitmap( openFileDialog1.FileName ) ;
}
catch ( Exception error )
{
  MessageBox.Show( "Error: Select An Image File!" ) ;
}
```

The PictureBoxSizeMode. **StretchImage** property will stretch, or shrink, a selected image to fit the **PictureBox** dimensions as a new Bitmap image.

7 Press **Start** or **F5** to run the application and call the system dialogs to choose program options

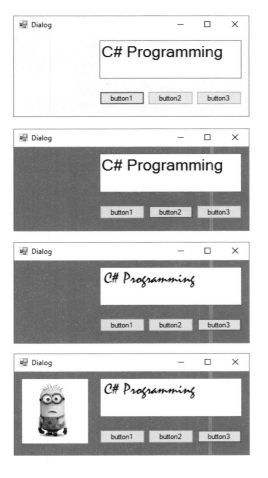

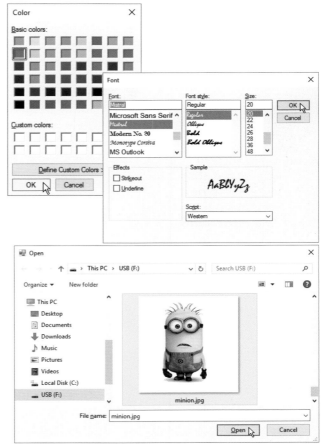

Creating application menus

Drop-down menus, toolbars, and status bars, like those found in most Windows applications, can easily be added to your own C# GUI applications from the Toolbox:

Jotter

1 Start a new **Windows Forms Application** project and find the **Menus & Toolbars** section of the Toolbox, then double-click the **MenuStrip** item to add it to the Form

2 Click the MenuStrip control's ▶ arrow button to open its **Smart Tag**, then select **Insert Standard Items**

Hot tip

Alternatively, you can create your own custom menus using the **Type Here** box instead of **Insert Standard Items**.

3 When the familiar headings and items have been added to the MenuStrip, right-click on any item and use the context menu to edit that item. Also, type new custom items into the **Type Here** box as required

4 In the Toolbox, double-click on the **ToolStrip** item to add it to the Form, then open its **Smart Tag** and once more select **Insert Standard Items**

5 When the familiar icon buttons have been added to the **ToolStrip**, right-click on any item and use the context menu to edit that item. Also add further custom items from the drop-down list as required

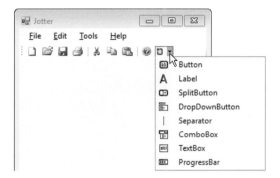

6 In the Toolbox, double-click on the **StatusStrip** item to add it to the Form

7 Select the **StatusLabel** item on the StatusStrip drop-down list, and set its text property to "Ready"

8 Add a **RichTextBox** control to the center of the Form, open its **Smart Tag** and select the option to **Dock in parent container**, then ensure that its **ScrollBars** property is set to **Both**

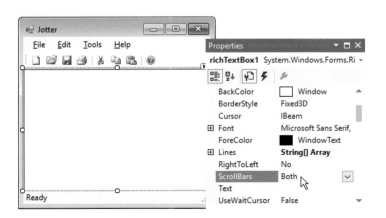

Making menus work

The menu items and toolbar buttons created on pages 146-147 will not truly function until you add code to make them work. For actions that appear both in a menu and on a button, you can create a method that can be called from the **Click** event-handler of the menu item and that of the button – to avoid duplication:

Jotter
(continued)

1 In Form Designer, click **File**, **New** to select the **New** menu item

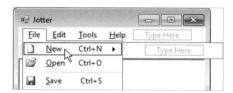

2 Double-click on the **New** menu item to open the **Code Editor** in its **Click** event-handler, and add this method call
newFile( ) ;

3 After the **Click** event-handler block, add this method to clear any existing text and display a status message
private void newFile( )
{
  richTextBox1.Text = null ;
  toolStripStatusLabel1.Text = "Ready" ;
}

4 Return to the **Form Designer**, then double-click on the **New** toolbar button to open the **Code Editor** in that event-handler, and add a call to the method above
newFile( ) ;

When you enable New, Open, and Save dialogs, keyboard shortcuts are already configured – try **Ctrl** + **N**, **Ctrl** + **S**, and **Ctrl** + **O** to test them.

5 Add an **OpenFileDialog** and **SaveFileDialog** component from the **Dialogs** section of the **Toolbox**

6 In the **Click** event-handlers of both the **Open** menu item and the **Open** toolbar button, add this method call
openFile( ) ;

...cont'd

7 After the **Click** event-handler blocks, add this method to load a plain text file
```
private void openFile( )
{
  openFileDialog1.Filter = "Text Files | *.txt" ;
  if ( openFileDialog1.ShowDialog( ) == DialogResult.OK )
  {
    richTextBox1.LoadFile( openFileDialog1.FileName ,
                      RichTextBoxStreamType.PlainText ) ;
  }
}
```

You can change the Filter to **"RichText | *.rtf"** and the RichTextBoxStreamType property to **.RichText** for files with embedded objects such as images.

8 In the **Click** event-handlers of both the **Save** menu item and the **Save** toolbar button, add this method call
```
saveFile( ) ;
```

9 After the **Click** event-handler blocks, add this method to save a plain text file
```
private void saveFile( )
{
  saveFileDialog1.Filter = "Text Files | *.txt" ;
  if ( saveFileDialog1.ShowDialog( ) == DialogResult.OK )
  {
    richTextBox1.SaveFile( saveFileDialog1.FileName ,
                      RichTextBoxStreamType.PlainText ) ;
  }
}
```

To make the **File**, **Exit** menu item functional, simply add the call **Application.Exit( )** ; to its **Click** event-handler.

10 Press **Start** or **F5** to run the application and test the functionality of the **New**, **Open**, and **Save** file menu items and toolbar buttons

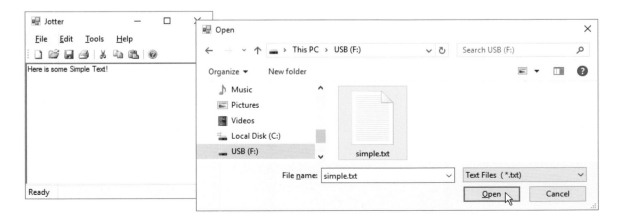

149

Importing audio resources

Sound files can be included within an application as a resource, in much the same way that image files can be imported as a resource, to enhance the application. These can then be played as required:

Sound

1 Start a new **Windows Forms Application** project and add a single **Button** control to the Form

2 Select **Project**, *ProjectName* **Properties** on the Menu Bar, to open the **Project Designer** window

It is advisable to use the **Project Designer** to remove a resource, rather than deleting it from **Solution Explorer**.

150

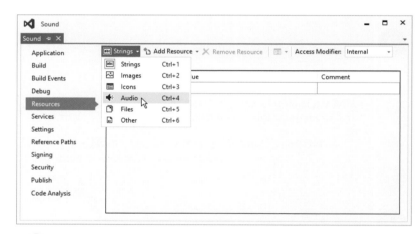

3 In **Project Designer**, select the **Resources** item in the left pane, then choose the **Audio** item from the drop-down list

4 Select the **Add Existing File...** item from the **Add Resource** drop-down list to launch the **Add existing file to resources** dialog

You can typically find the Windows sound files in the folder on your computer at **C:\Windows\Media**.

5 Browse to the location of the sound file you wish to add, then select the file and click the **Open** button

A sound can be played repeatedly using the **PlayLooping( )** method – and the loop can be ended with the **Stop( )** method.

6 The sound file now gets added to the **Resources** folder in **Solution Explorer** and appears in the **Resources** window of **Project Designer** – here, it's a file named **notify.wav**

7 Now, open the **Code Editor** and add a directive at the beginning of the page to make another C# class available
using System.Media ;

8 Double-click the **Button** control, then add this statement above its **Click** event-handler block to create an object
SoundPlayer notifier =
  new SoundPlayer(Properties.Resources.notify) ;

The sound file name only is dot-suffixed to **Properties.**Resources – without its file extension.

9 Now, add these statements inside the **Button** control's **Click** event-handler to show a message and play the sound
label1.Text = "Notifying..." ;
notifier.Play( ) ;

10 Press **Start** or **F5** to run the application and push the **Button** to hear the sound play

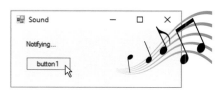

Summary

- The **Windows Forms Application** template in the New Project dialog is used to begin a Windows GUI project.

- The **Form Designer** window of the Visual Studio IDE is where you create the application's visual interface.

- The **Properties** window contains details of the item that is currently selected in the **Form Designer** window.

- The **Common Controls** section of the **Toolbox** contains a wide range of visual controls to build GUI applications.

- The **Code Editor** is used to create the code-behind page that determines how the application responds to interface events.

- When the user pushes a **Button** control, it creates a **Click** event to which its event-handler can respond.

- User input into a **TextBox** control can be assigned to a variable for use within the application.

- The user cannot modify text that appears on a **Label** control.

- Only one option can be checked in a **RadioButton** group, but any number of options can be checked in a **CheckBox** group.

- A **ListBox** control has an **Items** property that provides methods to add or remove items from the list it contains.

- The **Show( )** method of the MessageBox class accepts arguments to specify a message, caption, buttons, and icon.

- The **Dialogs** section of the **Toolbox** contains components that allow an application to use the Windows system dialogs.

- The **Menus & Toolbars** section of the **Toolbox** contains components that allow an application to include the familiar Windows system menu items.

- The **Menus & Toolbars** components will not truly function until code is added to their **Click** event-handlers.

- The **Project Designer** window can be used to import resources into an application project.

- A SoundPlayer object can be created using the **System.Media** class, and provides methods to handle audio resources.

11 Building an application

Planning the program

When creating a new application it is useful to spend some time planning its design. Clearly define the program's precise purpose, decide what application functionality will be required, then decide what interface components will be needed.

A plan for a simple application to pick numbers for a lottery game entry might look like this:

Program purpose

- The program will generate a series of six different random numbers in the range 1–59, and have the ability to be reset.

Functionality required

- A random number generator.
- A method to display six different random numbers.
- A method to clear the last series from display.

Components needed

- Six **Label** controls to display the series of numbers – one number per Label.
- One **Button** control to generate and display the numbers in the Label controls when this Button is clicked. This Button will not be enabled when numbers are on display.
- One **Button** control to clear the numbers on display in the Label controls when this Button is clicked. This Button will not be enabled when no numbers are on display.
- One **PictureBox** control to display a static image – just to enhance the appearance of the interface.

Omission of the planning stage can require time-consuming changes to be made later. It's better to "plan your work, then work your plan".

Toggle the value of a Button's **Enabled** property to steer the user. In this case, the application must be reset before a further series of numbers can be generated.

Having established a program plan means you can now create the application basics by adding the components needed to a Form:

1 Open the Visual Studio IDE and create a new **Windows Forms Application** project called "Lotto"

Lotto

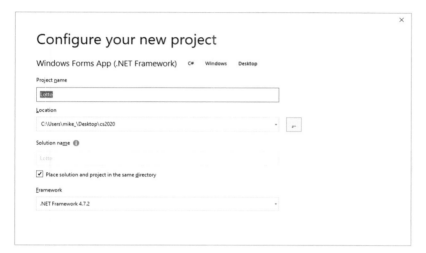

Configure your new project

Windows Forms App (.NET Framework)   C#   Windows   Desktop

Project name

Lotto

Location

C:\Users\mike_\Desktop\cs2020

Solution name ⓘ

Lotto

☑ Place solution and project in the same directory

Framework

.NET Framework 4.7.2

2 In the **Form Designer**, add six **Label** controls to the Form from the **Toolbox**

3 Now, add two **Button** controls and a **PictureBox** control to the Form

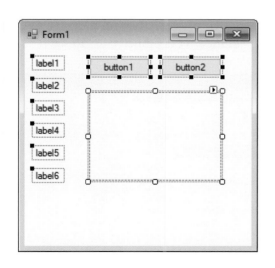

You can drag and drop items from the **Toolbox**, or double-click them to add them to the Form.

Assigning fixed properties

Having created the application basics on page 155, you can now assign static values using the **Properties** window:

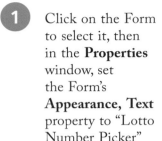

Lotto
(continued)

1 Click on the Form to select it, then in the **Properties** window, set the Form's **Appearance, Text** property to "Lotto Number Picker"

Properties	▾ □ ×
Form1 System.Windows.Forms.Form	
RightToLeftLayout	False
Text	**Lotto Number Picker**
UseWaitCursor	False
⊞ **Behavior**	
⊟ **Data**	

Don't forget

You can open the **Properties** window using the **F4** key, or by clicking **View**, **Properties Window** on the Menu Bar.

2 Select the first **Button** control, then in the **Properties** window, change its **Design, (Name)** property to **BtnPick**, and its **Appearance, Text** to "Get My Lucky Numbers"

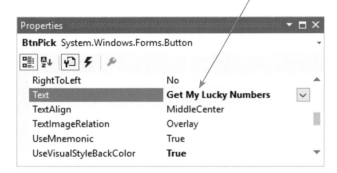

Properties	▾ □ ×
BtnPick System.Windows.Forms.Button	
RightToLeft	No
Text	**Get My Lucky Numbers**
TextAlign	MiddleCenter
TextImageRelation	Overlay
UseMnemonic	True
UseVisualStyleBackColor	**True**

Hot tip

The Label controls in this program will have their Text property values assigned dynamically at runtime – no initial properties are required.

3 Select the second **Button** control, then in the **Properties** window, change its **Design, (Name)** property to **BtnReset**, and its **Appearance, Text** property to "Reset"

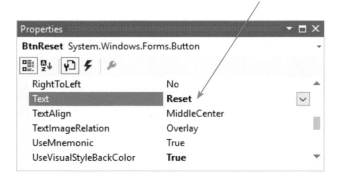

Properties	▾ □ ×
BtnReset System.Windows.Forms.Button	
RightToLeft	No
Text	**Reset**
TextAlign	MiddleCenter
TextImageRelation	Overlay
UseMnemonic	True
UseVisualStyleBackColor	**True**

4 Select the **PictureBox** control, then in the **Properties** window, click the **Appearance**, **Image** property ellipsis button to launch the **Select Resource** dialog

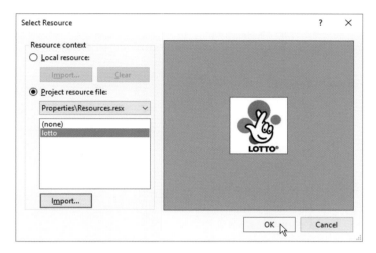

5 Click the **Import** button, browse to the image location, then click **OK** to import the image resource – this action automatically assigns it to the PictureBox's **Image** property

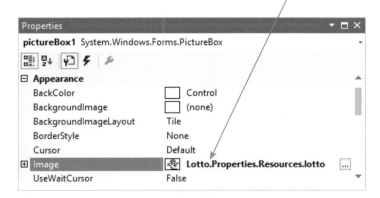

6 Click **File, Save Form1.cs** or press the **Ctrl + S** keys to save the changes made to the project form properties

Designing the layout

Having assigned fixed property values on pages 156-157, you can now design the interface layout.

The size of both the **PictureBox** control and the **BtnPick** control first needs to be adjusted to accommodate their content. This can easily be achieved by specifying an **AutoSize** value so that Visual Studio will automatically fit the control neatly around its content:

Lotto
(continued)

Hot tip

Alternatively, you can use the **Smart Tag** arrow button on a **PictureBox** control to set its **SizeMode** property.

Beware

Ensure that all PictureBox **Margin** properties are set to zero if you do not require margins around the image.

1. Select the **PictureBox** control, then in the **Properties** window, change its **Behavior, SizeMode** to **AutoSize**

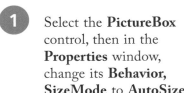

2. Select the **BtnPick** control, then in the **Properties** window, set its **Layout, AutoSize** property to **True**

3. See that the **PictureBox** control now snugly fits around the image, and the **BtnPick** control has expanded to fit its text

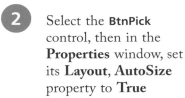

4. Hold down the left mouse button and drag around the Labels to select all **Label** controls

5. Now, click **View, Toolbars, Layout** to add the Layout toolbar to the Visual Studio menus

6. Click the **Align Tops** button to stack the Labels in a pile

7 Click the **Make Horizontal Spacing Equal** toolbar button to arrange the pile of Labels into a row

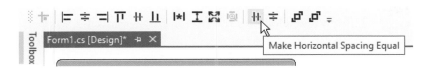

In this case, it does not matter in what order the Labels appear in the row.

8 Use the Form's right grab handle to extend its width to accommodate the row of Labels and **PictureBox**, then drag the row and both Buttons to the top-right of the Form

9 Drag the **PictureBox** control to the top-left of the Form, then use the Form's bottom grab handle to adjust its height to match that of the image

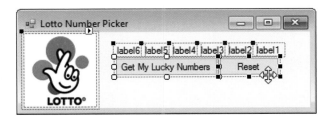

10 Use the **Snap Lines** that appear when you drag controls around the Form to position the row of Labels and the Buttons to make the interface look like the layout below

Avoid the temptation to change the default styles of form controls so they remain familiar to users.

11 Set the Form's **Window Style**, **MaximizeBox** and **MinimizeBox** properties to **False**, as maximize and minimize buttons are not required on this interface

Setting dynamic properties

Having designed the interface on pages 158-159, you can now add some functionality to dynamically set the initial **Text** properties of the **Label** controls and the initial **Button** states:

Lotto
(continued)

1 Click **View**, **Code** on the Menu Bar, or press **F7**, to open the **Code Editor** window

2 After the **Form1( )** constructor method block, add a new method block
private void Clear( )
{
   // Statements to be inserted here (Steps 4-8).
}

3 With the cursor inside the new method block, press **Ctrl** + **J**, to open the **IntelliSense** pop-up window

4 Scroll down the list of items in the **IntelliSense** window and double-click on the **label1** item to add it into the **Clear( )** method block

The technique described here demonstrates how to use **IntelliSense** – but you can, of course, just type the code directly.

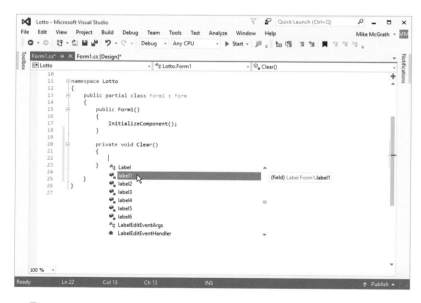

5 Type a period, then double-click the **Text** item when the **IntelliSense** window reappears, to add that code

6 Now, type = "..." ; to complete the line so it reads like this:
label1.Text = "..." ;

7 Repeat this procedure for the other **Label** controls – so that the **Clear( )** method assigns each an ellipsis string

8 With the cursor inside the **Clear( )** method block, use **IntelliSense** in the same way, to add these two lines:
BtnPick.Enabled = true ;
BtnReset.Enabled = false ;

This completes the **Clear( )** method functionality by setting the **Button** states. All that remains is to add a call to the **Clear( )** method to execute all of its instructions when the program starts.

9 In the **Form Designer**, double-click on the Form to open the **Code Editor** in its **Load** event-handler, then press **Ctrl + J** to open the **IntelliSense** window

10 Scroll down the list in the **IntelliSense** window and double-click on the **Clear** item you have just created, to add a call statement in the **Load** event-handler

Type "Intellisense" into the Quick Launch box at the top of the Visual Studio window to discover the IntelliSense Menus and Options.

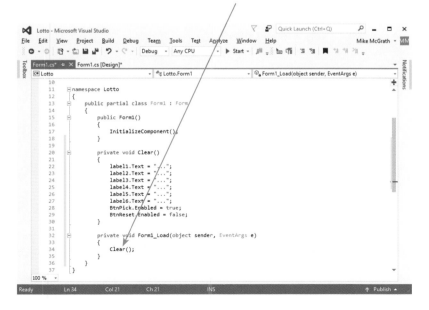

You could add some comments to make the code more friendly.

Lotto
(continued)

Adding runtime function

Having created code to initialize dynamic properties on pages 160-161, you can now add runtime functionality to respond to clicks on the **Button** controls:

1 In the **Form Designer**, double-click on the **BtnReset Button** control to open the **Code Editor** in its **Click** event-handler, then add this method call
Clear( ) ;

This is all that is needed to provide dynamic functionality for the **BtnReset** control. The main dynamic functionality of this application is provided by the **BtnPick** control, which requires an instance of a Random class, random number generator object:

2 In the **Form Designer**, double-click on the **BtnPick Button** control to open the **Code Editor** in its **Click** event-handler

3 In the **Click** event-handler block, add this statement to create a random number generator object
Random **rnd = new** Random**( ) ;**

Hot tip

The random number generator is used here to generate random values between zero and 58 to shuffle array elements.

4 Next, add a statement to create an array of 59 elements to store a sequence of numbers
int [ ] seq = new int[59] ;

5 Now, add a loop to fill the array elements (index 0 to 58) with integer values 1 to 59
```
for ( int i = 1 ; i < 60 ; i++ )
{
  seq[ i - 1 ] = i ;
}
```

6 Add a second loop to shuffle the values within all the array elements – an algorithm to randomize their order
```
for ( int i = 0 ; i < 59 ; i++ )
{
  int j = ( rnd.Next( ) % 59 ) ;
  int k = seq[ i ] ; seq[ i ] = seq[ j ] ; seq[ j ] = k ;
}
```

Don't forget

You don't need to understand in detail the algorithm that is used to shuffle the values.

...cont'd

Next, add the following lines to display the numbers contained in array elements 1-6 in the **Label** controls
```
label1.Text = seq[ 1 ].ToString( ) ;
label2.Text = seq[ 2 ].ToString( ) ;
label3.Text = seq[ 3 ].ToString( ) ;
label4.Text = seq[ 4 ].ToString( ) ;
label5.Text = seq[ 5 ].ToString( ) ;
label6.Text = seq[ 6 ].ToString( ) ;
```

Now, add these two lines to set the **Button** states ready to reset the application
```
BtnPick.Enabled = false ;
BtnReset.Enabled = true ;
```

The **Label** controls can only contain **string** values, so the **int** numeric values must be converted.

Add comments for others examining the code, and for yourself when revisiting the code later

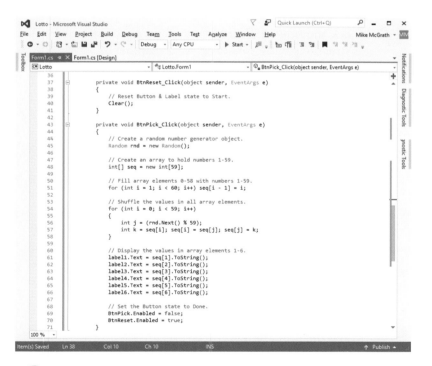

You can have Visual Studio nicely format your code by selecting **Edit**, **Advanced**, **Format Document**, or using the keyboard shortcut shown there – typically, this is **Ctrl + K, Ctrl + D**.

Click **File, Save All** or press the **Ctrl + Shift + S** keys to save the changes made to the project code-behind page

Testing the program

Having worked through the program plan on the previous pages, the components needed and functionality required have now been added to the application – so it's ready to be tested:

Lotto
(continued)

 1 Click the **Start** button, or press **F5**, to run the application then examine its initial start-up appearance

The Form's **Load** event-handler has set the initial dynamic values of each **Label** control and disabled the reset button as required.

2 Click the **BtnPick Button** control to execute the instructions within its **Click** event-handler

Hot tip

Notice that no number is repeated in any series.

A series of numbers within the desired range is displayed, and the **Button** states have changed as required – a further series of numbers cannot be generated until the application has been reset.

3 Make a note of the numbers generated in this first series for comparison later

4 Click the **BtnReset** control to execute the instructions within that **Click** event-handler and see the application return to its initial start-up appearance as required

164

5 Click the **BtnPick Button** control again to execute its **Click** event-handler code a second time

Another series of numbers within the desired range is displayed and are different to those in the first series when compared – good, the numbers are being randomized as required.

6 Click the **Stop Debugging** button, then click the **Start** button to restart the application and click the **BtnPick Button** control once more

The generated numbers in this first series of numbers are different to those noted in the first series the last time the application ran – great, the random number generator is not repeating the same sequence of number series each time the application runs.

Remember that this application interface has no minimize or maximize buttons because their properties were set to false – see page 159, Step 11.

Alternatively, you can click the app's X button to close the application and stop debugging.

Publishing the application

Having satisfactorily tested the application on pages 164-165, you can now create a standalone version that can be executed outside the Visual Studio IDE, and that can be distributed to others for deployment elsewhere.

Lotto
(continued)

1 Click **Project** on the Menu Bar, choose **Lotto Properties**, **Signing**, check the **Sign the ClickOnce manifests** box, then click **Select from Store...** and choose a certificate

Hot tip

Applications signing is optional, but does verify authentication. Find more details online at docs.microsoft.com/en-us/visualstudio/ide/how-to-sign-application-and-deployment-manifests

2 Click **Build**, **Build Lotto**, then click **Build**, **Publish Lotto** to launch the **Publish Wizard** dialog

3 Use the wizard's **Browse** button to select a location where you wish to publish the application – the chosen location shown here is the root directory of removable drive **F:**

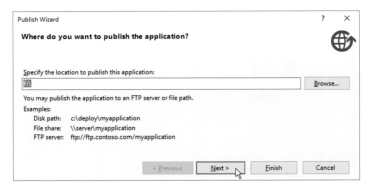

Hot tip

When choosing a publish location, use the **Create New Folder** button in the **File System** dialog to make a folder to contain all the application files.

4 Click the **Next** button, then select whether the user will install the application from a website, network, or portable media such as CD, DVD, or removable drive – in this case, accept the default portable media option

5 Click the **Next** button, then select whether the installer should check for application updates – accept the default option not to check for updates in this case

6 Click the **Next** button to move to the final dialog page, confirm the listed choices, then click the **Finish** button to publish the application at the specified location

Each time you publish an application, its version number is automatically incremented – 1.0.0.0, 1.0.0.1, 1.0.0.2, etc.

The **Publish Wizard** generates a number of files, including a familiar "setup.exe" executable installer.

7 Move the portable media to the system where it is to be deployed, then run **setup.exe** to install the application

When the application is installed on the client system, a shortcut is automatically added to the **Start menu**, which can be used to launch the application. The user can then run the release version of the application just as it performed during testing of its debug version in the Visual Studio IDE.

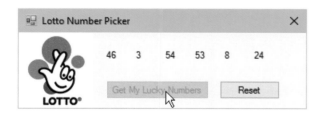

An application cannot be published unless it has been built first.

The installer also adds an item to the client system's **Add/Remove Programs** list, which can be used to uninstall the application – just like any other Windows program.

Summary

- Always make an initial program plan, to avoid the need for time-consuming changes later.

- A program plan should clearly define the program purpose, functionality required, and components needed.

- Fixed properties that will not change when the application is running can be set at design time in the **Properties** Window.

- The **Import** button in the **Select Resources** dialog can automatically assign an image to a **PictureBox** control.

- An **AutoSize** property value makes Visual Studio automatically fit a control neatly around its content.

- The Form Designer's **Layout** toolbar contains useful features to quickly align and space multiple interface controls.

- **Snap Lines** help you to easily align a selected control to others in the interface at design time.

- Setting a Form's **Window Style**, **MaximizeBox**, and **MinimizeBox** properties to **False** removes those buttons.

- Dynamic properties that will change when the application is running can be initialized with the Form's **Load** event-handler.

- The pop-up **IntelliSense** window lets you easily add program code when using the **Code Editor**.

- Runtime functionality responds to user actions by changing dynamic properties.

- A **Debug** version of an application allows its functionality to be tested as the application is being created in text format.

- The **Build** process compiles a **Release** version of an application in binary format.

- The **Publish** process creates a final **Release** version with an installer so the application can be deployed elsewhere.

- Applications created with the Visual Studio IDE can be installed and uninstalled just like other Windows applications.

12 Targeting devices

Starting a Universal project

Windows 10 introduced the **Universal Windows Platform (UWP)** that enables you to create a single application that will run on any modern Windows-based device – phone, tablet, or PC.

The interface layout of a UWP application uses the **eXtensible Application Markup Language** (XAML) to specify components.

In order to develop apps for the UWP you should be running the latest version of Windows 10, and your Visual Studio IDE must include the Universal Windows Platform development tools:

Beware

The example in this chapter is for Visual Studio 2019 on Windows 10 – it won't work in earlier Windows editions.

Universal

1. Click **Visual Studio Installer** on the Apps menu, then click the **Modify** button on the Installer dialog

2. Select the **Workloads** tab, and ensure that the box is checked for the Universal Windows Platform development option – indicating this is installed

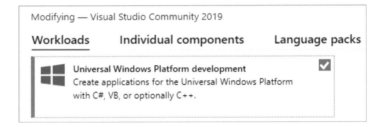

Modifying — Visual Studio Community 2019

Workloads	Individual components	Language packs

Universal Windows Platform development
Create applications for the Universal Windows Platform with C#, VB, or optionally C++. ☑

Hot tip

A UWP application is also known as a "UWA" – Universal Windows Application.

3. If the box was not already checked, this item will need to be installed, so check the box now

4. Click the **Modify** button at the bottom-right of the Installer dialog to download and install the Universal Windows Platform development tools

Don't forget

Depending upon your choices when you installed Visual Studio, you may see the options checked when the installer launches, to indicate you already have the Universal Windows App Development Tools.

5. Next, select **File**, **New**, **Project** and create a new **Blank App (Universal Windows)** project called "Universal"

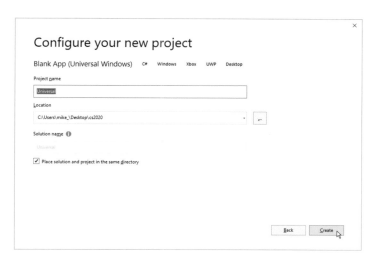

In Windows 10 you should ensure that the **Developer Mode** option is enabled in **Settings**, **Update & Security**, **For developers**.

6 Click **OK** to accept the suggested version options

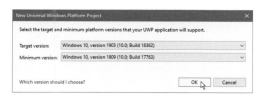

7 After Visual Studio creates the new project, select **View**, **Solution Explorer** to examine the generated files:

- A set of logo images in an **Assets** folder.

- Internal XAML and C# files for the **App**.

- XAML and C# files for the **MainPage** – here is where you will create interface components and functional code.

- Other miscellaneous **Package** files.

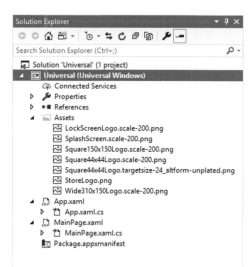

These files are essential to all UWP apps using C#, and exist in every project Visual Studio creates to target the Universal Windows Platform with C#.

Inserting page components

Visual Studio provides a two-part window to insert interface components into a UWP app. This comprises a **Design** view of the components, and a **XAML** view for the XAML code:

Universal
(continued)

XAML is pronounced "zammel".

There is a **Toolbox** that lets you add components onto the canvas, but you will need to edit them in the XAML code later. In this example, the components are created in XAML code from the very start.

Explore these buttons to change the magnification and grid characteristics.

1 Open **Solution Explorer** then double-click on **MainPage.xaml** – to launch the two-part window

2 See that, by default, the **Design** view may display a blank canvas in **Portrait** mode

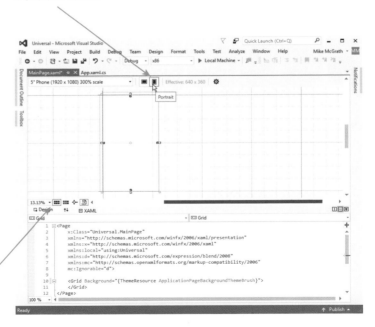

3 Click the adjacent button in **Design** view to change the blank canvas to **Landscape** mode

...cont'd

4 Now, see that by default, the **XAML** view reveals there are **<Grid> </Grid>** tags – this is the root element of the canvas in which you can add component elements

Component elements are best nested within a **<StackPanel>** element, as this can be given an **x:Name** for reference in functional code, and an **Orientation** attribute to specify the direction in which the nested elements should appear. Common component elements include **<Image>**, **<TextBox>**, **<TextBlock>** (label), and **<Button>**. Several **<StackPanel>** elements can be nested within each other to determine the **Horizontal** and **Vertical** layout of components:

5 Insert elements between the root **<Grid> </Grid>** tags, so the **XAML** view code looks precisely like this:

Hot tip

The **x:** prefix before the **Name** attribute refers to the XAML schema used by UWP apps.

```xml
10  <Grid Background="{ThemeResource ApplicationPageBackgroundThemeBrush}">
11
12      <StackPanel x:Name="MainStack" Orientation="Horizontal">
13
14          <Image x:Name="Image" Width="200" Height="200" />
15
16          <StackPanel x:Name="Controls" Orientation="Vertical" VerticalAlignment="Center">
17
18              <StackPanel x:Name="Labels" Orientation="Horizontal">
19                  <TextBlock x:Name="textBlock1" Text="TextBlock"/>
20                  <TextBlock x:Name="textBlock2" Text="TextBlock"/>
21                  <TextBlock x:Name="textBlock3" Text="TextBlock"/>
22                  <TextBlock x:Name="textBlock4" Text="TextBlock"/>
23                  <TextBlock x:Name="textBlock5" Text="TextBlock"/>
24                  <TextBlock x:Name="textBlock6" Text="TextBlock"/>
25              </StackPanel>
26
27              <StackPanel x:Name="Buttons" Orientation="Horizontal">
28                  <Button x:Name="BtnPick" Content="Button"/>
29                  <Button x:Name="BtnReset" Content="Button"/>
30              </StackPanel>
31
32          </StackPanel>
33
34      </StackPanel>
35
36  </Grid>
```

Hot tip

The outer **<StackPanel>** is a horizontal layout containing an **<Image>** and a nested **<StackPanel>**. The nested **<StackPanel>** is a vertical layout containing two further **<StackPanel>** elements that each display their components horizontally.

6 As you add the component elements in **XAML** view, they appear in the **Design** view until it looks like this:

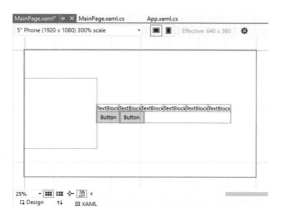

Don't forget

Notice that each **<TextBlock>** element has a **Text** attribute that can be referenced in functional code – for example, **textBlock1.Text**.

173

Importing program assets

In order to have a XAML **<Image>** component display a graphic, an image file first needs to be added to the projects **Assets** folder. It can then be assigned to a **Source** attribute of the **<Image>** tag:

Universal
(continued)

1 Open **Solution Explorer**, then right-click on the **Assets** folder and choose **Add** from the context menu

2 Now, choose **Existing Item...** from the next context menu – to open an **Add Existing Item** dialog box

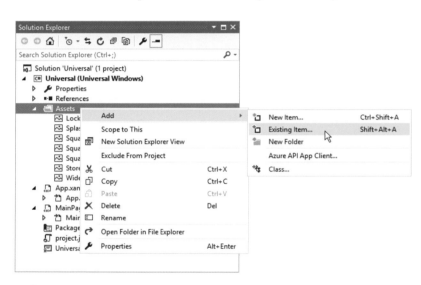

3 In the **Add Existing Item** dialog, browse to the location of an image, then select the file and click the **Add** button

Hot tip

An image for display may be in any popular file format – such as **.bmp**, **.gif**, **.jpg**, **.png**, or **.tif**.

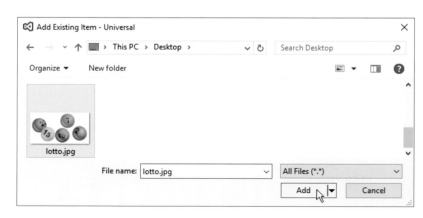

4 In **Solution Explorer**, the selected image file now appears in the project's **Asset** folder

5 Select the Image component in **Designer** view, then click **View**, **Properties** to reveal its properties

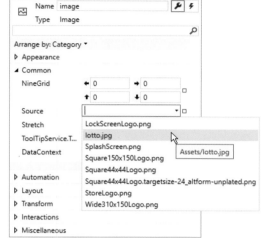

Explore the **Appearance** and **Transform** options in an image's **Properties** window, to discover how you can modify how it will be displayed.

6 In the **Properties** window, expand the **Common** category, then click the **Source** item's arrow button and select the added image from the drop-down list

7 The image now appears in the **Design** view, and its path gets added to the **XAML** view code and **Source** property

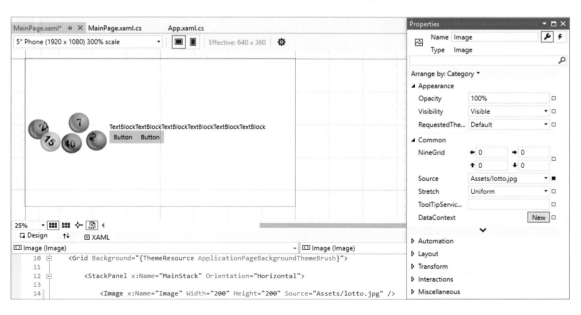

Designing the layout

To complete the app's layout, design attributes can be added to the XAML element tags to specify what they will display and precisely where in the interface they will appear:

1 Open **MainPage.xaml**, then add two attributes to the outer **<StackPanel>** element to fix its position
HorizontalAlignment = "Left" VerticalAlignment = "Top"

2 Next, edit the **<Image>** element by modifying the initial assigned value of 200 – to increase its width
Width = "300"

3 Now, add an attribute to the nested **<StackPanel>** element to fix its position
VerticalAlignment = "Center"

4 Then, edit all six **<TextBlock>** elements alike, to specify their initial content, width, and margin on all four sides
Text = "..." Width = "20" Margin = "15"
Text = "..." Width = "20" Margin = "15"
Text = "..." Width = "20" Margin = "15"
Text = "..." Width = "20" Margin = "15"
Text = "..." Width = "20" Margin = "15"
Text = "..." Width = "20" Margin = "15"

5 Edit the first **<Button>** element to rename it, and specify its button label content and margin on all four sides
x:Name = "BtnPick" Content = "Get My Lucky Numbers"
Margin = "15"

6 Edit the second **<Button>** element to rename it and specify its button label content
x:Name = "BtnReset" Content = "Reset"

7 Finally, add an attribute to each respective **<Button>** element to specify their initial state
IsEnabled = "True"
IsEnabled = "False"

A single **Margin** value sets all four margins around that component. You can specify two values to set left & right, top & bottom margins – e.g. **Margin = "10,30"**. Alternatively, you can specify four values to set left,top,right,bottom margins individually – e.g. **Margin = "10,30,10,50"**.

...cont'd

The order in which the attributes appear in each element is unimportant, but the elements within the **MainPage.xaml** file should now look similar to the screenshot below:

```
11
12      <StackPanel x:Name="MainStack" HorizontalAlignment="Left" VerticalAlignment="top" Orientation="Horizontal" >
13
14          <Image x:Name="Image" Width="300" Height="200" Source="Assets/lotto.jpg" />
15
16          <StackPanel x:Name="Controls" Orientation="Vertical" VerticalAlignment="Center">
17
18              <StackPanel x:Name="Labels" Orientation="Horizontal">
19                  <TextBlock x:Name="textBlock1" Text="..." Width="20" Margin="15"/>
20                  <TextBlock x:Name="textBlock2" Text="..." Width="20" Margin="15"/>
21                  <TextBlock x:Name="textBlock3" Text="..." Width="20" Margin="15"/>
22                  <TextBlock x:Name="textBlock4" Text="..." Width="20" Margin="15"/>
23                  <TextBlock x:Name="textBlock5" Text="..." Width="20" Margin="15"/>
24                  <TextBlock x:Name="textBlock6" Text="..." Width="20" Margin="15"/>
25              </StackPanel>
26
27              <StackPanel x:Name="Buttons" Orientation="Horizontal">
28                  <Button x:Name="BtnPick" Content="Get My Lucky Numbers" Margin="15" IsEnabled="True"/>
29                  <Button x:Name="BtnReset" Content="Reset" IsEnabled="False"/>
30              </StackPanel>
31
32          </StackPanel>
33
34      </StackPanel>
```

You can optionally add **Margin = "0"** attributes to explicitly require elements to have no margin width.

As you make changes to the **XAML** view code, the component layout gets changed accordingly in the **Design** view, and should now look like this:

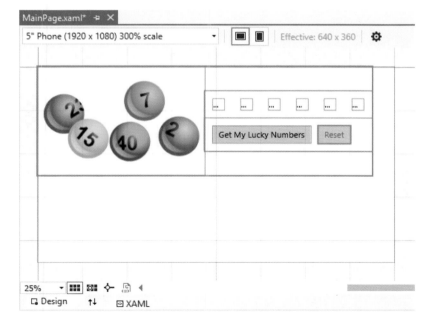

The **Design** view shows the components' initial state – the Reset button appears grayed out, as it is not enabled.

Adding runtime function

Having completed the application component layout with XAML elements on pages 176-177, you are now ready to add functionality with C# programming code:

Universal
(continued)

Hot tip

The randomizer routine uses exactly the same logic as that of the **Windows Forms Application** example – see page 162.

Don't forget

There is no **Label** component in UWP apps; it is called a **TextBlock** instead.

Beware

There is no **Enabled** property in UWP apps; it is called **IsEnabled** instead.

1 In **Design** view, double-click on the **BtnPick** button

2 The **MainPage.xaml.cs** code-behind page opens in the **Code Editor** at a generated **BtnPick_Click** event-handler

3 In the **BtnPick_Click** event-handler block, insert these statements to create a randomized array of integers between 1 and 59

```
Random rnd = new Random( ) ;
int [ ] seq = new int[ 59 ] ;
for ( int i = 1 ; i < 60 ; i++ ) seq[ i - 1 ] = i ;
for ( int i = 0 ; i < 59 ; i++ )
{
  int j = ( rnd.Next( ) % 59 ) ;
  int k = seq[ i ] ; seq[ i ] = seq[ j ] ; seq[ j ] = k ;
}
// Statements to be inserted here (Steps 4-5).
```

4 Next, insert statements to assign six array element values to the **<TextBlock>** components

```
textBlock1.Text = seq[ 1 ].ToString( ) ;
textBlock2.Text = seq[ 2 ].ToString( ) ;
textBlock3.Text = seq[ 3 ].ToString( ) ;
textBlock4.Text = seq[ 4 ].ToString( ) ;
textBlock5.Text = seq[ 5 ].ToString( ) ;
textBlock6.Text = seq[ 6 ].ToString( ) ;
```

5 Next, insert statements to set the **<Button>** states

```
BtnPick.IsEnabled = false ;
BtnReset.IsEnabled = true ;
```

6 Return to **MainPage.xaml**, then in **Design** view, double-click on the **BtnReset** button

7 The **MainPage.xaml.cs** code-behind page opens in the **Code Editor** at a generated **BtnReset_Click** event-handler

8 In the **BtnReset_Click** event-handler block, insert statements to assign strings to the **<TextBlock>** components
```
textBlock1.Text = "..." ;
textBlock2.Text = "..." ;
textBlock3.Text = "..." ;
textBlock4.Text = "..." ;
textBlock5.Text = "..." ;
textBlock6.Text = "..." ;
// Statements to be inserted here (Step 9).
```

The **BtnReset** button simply returns the **<TextBox>** and **<Button>** components to their original states.

9 Finally, insert statements to set the **<Button>** states
```
BtnPick.IsEnabled = true ;
BtnReset.IsEnabled = false ;
```

The **MainPage.xaml.cs** code-behind page should now look like the screenshot below:

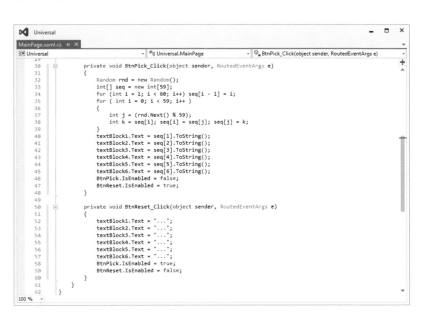

Notice that the first **for** loop contains only one statement to be executed on each iteration, so braces are not required.

179

10 Return to the **MainPage.xaml** file, then in **XAML** view, see that attributes have been automatically added to the **<Button>** elements to call the event-handler code

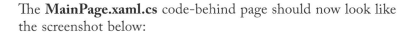

Testing the program

Having added functionality with C# code on pages 178-179, you are now ready to test the program for two devices:

Universal
(continued)

1 On the Visual Studio standard toolbar, select the **Debug** for **x64** architecture and **Local Machine** options, then click the **Start** button to run the app for a PC device

2 Wait while the application gets built and loaded, then click the buttons to try out their functionality

Don't forget

You must have your PC set to **Developer Mode** in **Settings**, **Update & Security**, **For developers**.

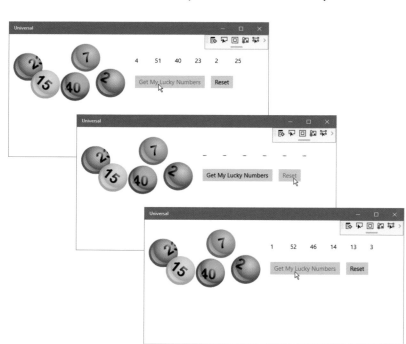

The app looks good on PC devices – numbers are being randomized and the button states are changing as required.

3 Now, on the Visual Studio standard toolbar, select **Debug**, **Stop Debugging** to exit the running program

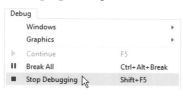

4 On the Visual Studio standard toolbar, select **Debug** for **x86** architecture and **Simulator** options, then click the **Start** button to run the app for a mobile device

Test on the simulator with lowest memory and smallest screen, and it should be fine running on those simulators with better features.

5 Wait while the simulator starts up – this takes a while

6 When the application gets built and loaded, you see the controls are not visible – so you can't try out their functionality!

7 What's going on here? Click the simulator's **Rotate** button to flip it over to Landscape orientation and look for clues

The simulator is a virtual machine that will only run on Windows 10 Pro, Windows 10 Enterprise, or Windows 10 Education editions – it will NOT run on the Windows 10 Home edition.

8 Ah-ha! Some of the controls are now visible, but this is unsatisfactory – adjustments will be needed to the interface layout so the app looks good on mobile devices

9 Again, on the Visual Studio standard toolbar, select **Debug**, **Stop Debugging** to exit the running program

181

Adjusting the interface

The app test for mobile devices on pages 180-181 failed to satisfactorily present the controls, as the interface is too wide for small screen devices. Happily, the interface can be made to adapt to different screen sizes so it can also look good on mobile devices. The adaptation relies upon recognizing the screen size and changing the orientation of a **<StackPanel>** element in **XAML** for narrow screen devices:

Universal
(continued)

Hot tip

XAML code recognizes the same **<!-- -->** comment tags that are used in HTML code.

182

1 Open **MainPage.xaml**, then in **XAML** view add these elements immediately below the opening **<Grid>** element and before the component elements

```
<VisualStateManager.VisualStateGroups>
  <VisualStateGroup>

  <!-- Elements to be inserted here (Steps 2-3) -->

  </VisualStateGroup>
</VisualStateManager.VisualStateGroups>
```

2 Next, insert elements to recognize wide screens

```
<VisualState x:Name = "wideState" >

  <VisualState.StateTriggers>
    <AdaptiveTrigger MinWindowWidth = "641" />
  </VisualState.StateTriggers>

</VisualState>
```

Don't forget

Remember that the outer **<StackPanel>** in this app contains an **<Image>** and a nested **<StackPanel>** displayed horizontally, side by side. If displayed vertically, they should appear one above the other.

3 Now, insert elements to recognize narrow screens, and to change the **Orientation** of the outer **<StackPanel>**

```
<VisualState x:Name = "narrowState" >

  <VisualState.StateTriggers>
    <AdaptiveTrigger MinWindowWidth = "0" />
  </VisualState.StateTriggers>

  <VisualState.Setters>
    <Setter
     Target = "MainStack.Orientation" Value = "Vertical" />
  </VisualState.Setters>

</VisualState>
```

The beginning of the **MainPage.xaml** file should now look similar to the screenshot at the top of the next page:

```
10    <Grid Background="{ThemeResource ApplicationPageBackgroundThemeBrush}">
11
12        <VisualStateManager.VisualStateGroups>
13            <VisualStateGroup>
14                <VisualState x:Name="wideState">
15                    <VisualState.StateTriggers>
16                        <AdaptiveTrigger MinWindowWidth="641"/>
17                    </VisualState.StateTriggers>
18                </VisualState>
19                <VisualState x:Name="narrowState">
20                    <VisualState.StateTriggers>
21                        <AdaptiveTrigger MinWindowWidth="0"/>
22                    </VisualState.StateTriggers>
23                    <VisualState.Setters>
24                        <Setter Target="MainStack.Orientation" Value="Vertical" />
25                    </VisualState.Setters>
26                </VisualState>
27            </VisualStateGroup>
28        </VisualStateManager.VisualStateGroups>
```

Hot tip

You can have Visual Studio nicely format the XAML code by pressing **Ctrl** + **K**, **Ctrl** + **D**.

4 Select **x64** and **Local Machine** to run the app for a PC device once more – it still looks and functions well

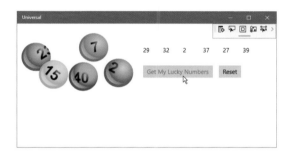

5 Now, select **x86** and **Local Machine** to run the app for a mobile device – reduce the window width to see the layout now automatically change to suit a narrow screen

Beware

Although an app may work well on an emulator, it is recommended you always test on actual devices before deployment.

Deploying the application

Having tested the app on your PC it can now be tested on a real device before deployment:

Universal
(continued)

1 On a Windows 10 device, select **Developer mode** from the **Settings**, **Update & Security**, **For developers** menu

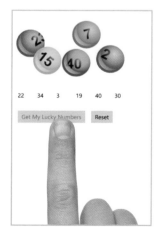

2 Next, connect the device to your PC via a USB socket

3 On the Visual Studio toolbar, select the **Debug** for **ARM** architecture and **Device** options, then click the **Start** button to run the app on the connected device

Hot tip

You can choose the **Remote Machine** option to test via a network connection.

4 Wait while the application gets built and loaded, then tap the buttons to try out their functionality

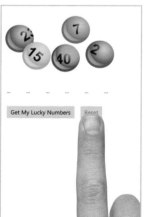

The app looks good, numbers are being randomized, and the button states are changing as required – the app can be deployed.

5 Remove the **Debug** version of the app from the device

6 In **Solution Explorer**, add logo images to the **Assets** folder, then double-click on **Package.appmanifest** and add them to **Visual Assets**

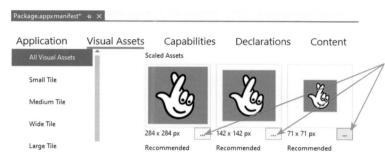

Hot tip

Add three logo images to the **Assets** folder of the required sizes, then click these buttons to select them to be the app tiles. You can also add tile images, a Splash Screen image, or select the **Application** tab and change the app's **Display name** – to "Lucky Numbers", for example.

185

7 On the Visual Studio toolbar, select the **Release** for **ARM** architecture and **Device** options, then click **Build**, **Deploy Solution** to build and install the **Release** version

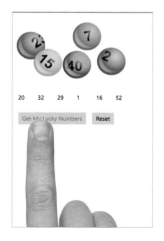

Hot tip

You can use your C# programming skills to build apps for Android and iOS with Visual Studio and Xamarin. Discover more online at **dotnet.microsoft.com/ apps/xamarin**

Summary

- The **Universal Windows Platform** (UWP) enables a single app to run on any modern Windows-based device.

- The **eXtensible Application Markup Language** (XAML) is used to specify components and layout on UWP apps.

- The **Universal Windows App Development Tools** are needed in order to develop UWP apps.

- The **Blank App (Universal Windows)** template can be used to create a new UWP project.

- Visual Studio provides a graphical **Design** view and a text code **XAML** view for the **MainPage.xaml** file.

- Component elements can be placed within XAML **<StackPanel>** elements to arrange their orientation.

- Image files can be added to the **Assets** folder and assigned to XAML **<Image>** elements for display on the interface.

- Space can be added around a component by adding a **Margin** attribute and assigned value within its element tag.

- Functional C# programming code can be added to the **MainPage.xaml.cs** code-behind page.

- The **Developer Mode** setting must be enabled in the Windows 10 options in order to develop and test UWP apps.

- A UWP app can be tested in **Debug** mode on the **Local Machine**, a **Simulator**, and a connected **Device**.

- The interface of a UWP app can adapt to different screen sizes by changing the orientation of **<StackPanel>** elements.

- Image files can be added to the **Assets** folder for assignment as logos in the **Package.appmanifest** window.

- The **Release** version can be deployed by selecting the target configuration, then using the **Build**, **Deploy Solution** menu.

Index

189